HARTLINE
Investment Corporation

Knowing successful wealth building strategies
is strongly enhanced by having statistical support
available in this book. It can give you the conviction
necessary to keep your commitment to the right path.

Best Wishes,

Bill Hart

D1266227

GET RICH,
STAY RICH,
PASS IT ON

GET RICH, STAY RICH, PASS IT ON

The Wealth Accumulation Secrets of America's Richest Families

CATHERINE S. MCBREEN

and GEORGE H. WALPER, JR.

PORTFOLIO

PORTFOLIO
Published by Penguin Group
Penguin Group (USA) Inc., 375 Hudson Street, New York, New York 10014, U.S.A.
Penguin Group (Canada), 90 Eglinton Avenue East, Suite 700,
Toronto, Ontario, Canada M4P 2Y3 (a division of Pearson Penguin Canada Inc.)
Penguin Books Ltd., 80 Strand, London WC2R 0RL, England
Penguin Ireland, 25 St. Stephen's Green, Dublin 2, Ireland (a division of Penguin Books Ltd)
Penguin Books Australia Ltd, 250 Camberwell Road, Camberwell,
Victoria 3124, Australia (a division of Pearson Australia Group Pty Ltd)
Penguin Books India Pvt Ltd, 11 Community Centre, Panchsheel Park,
New Delhi - 110 017, India
Penguin Books (NZ), 67 Apollo Drive, Rosedale, North Shore 0745,
Auckland, New Zealand (a division of Pearson New Zealand Ltd.)
Penguin Books (South Africa) (Pty) Ltd, 24 Sturdee Avenue,
Rosebank, Johannesburg 2196, South Africa

Penguin Books Ltd, Registered Offices: 80 Strand, London WC2R 0RL, England

First published in 2007 by Portfolio, a member of Penguin Group (USA) Inc.

1 3 5 7 9 10 8 6 4 2

Copyright © Catherine S. McBreen and George H. Walper, Jr., 2007
All rights reserved

Charts and graphs courtesy of Spectrem Group

PUBLISHER'S NOTE
This publication is designed to provide accurate and authoritative information in regard to the
subject matter covered. It is sold with the understanding that the publisher is not engaged in
rendering legal, accounting or other professional services. If you require legal advice or other
expert assistance, you should seek the services of a competent professional.

LIBRARY OF CONGRESS CATALOGING-IN-PUBLICATION DATA
McBreen, Catherine S.
Get rich, stay rich, pass it on : the wealth-accumulation secrets of America's richest families /
Catherine S. McBreen and George H. Walper, Jr.
p.   cm.
Includes index.
ISBN 978-1-59184-175-3
1. Wealth—United States. 2. Rich people—United States. 3. Millionaires—United States.
4. Inheritance and succession—United States. I. Walper, George H. II. Title.
HC110.W4M39 2007
332.024'01—dc22   2007005358

Printed in the United States of America
Set in Fairfield Light
Designed by Sabrina Bowers

To our children, the true treasure of our lives,
to whom we hope to pass on everything we gain from having
uncovered the secrets in this book . . .

Brooke Walper
Callie McBreen
Paul McBreen
Stacia McBreen
Tatum McBreen

CONTENTS

GET RICH,
STAY RICH,
PASS IT ON

A NEW STANDARD OF WEALTH

You may be richer than you think.

There's a new standard of wealth today, and a great many people who make the grade don't even know they're members of the club.

This new standard isn't just about living well—having enough to do pretty much anything, go pretty much anywhere, or buy just about anything. It isn't just about security, either—about owning every protection and hedge to guarantee a comfortable retirement for yourself. The new standard of wealth is about much more.

It is about having all of that *plus* the great bonus benefit of becoming rich—namely, the chance to leave a legacy of wealth to your children or heirs, to their children, and to the generations to come.

Think of it as a kind of perpetual wealth—enough wealth to keep you rich through your lifetime and to keep the heirs you will never meet rich forever. Such a legacy is within the reach of most people today, and most of them don't even know it.

Such a new measure of wealth may be within your reach, too—if only you know how to get it. That's why we wrote this book. It will tell you how.

RICH? AFFLUENT? GETTING THERE?

Are you worth $5 million—not including the house you live in? Some 1,140,000 American households are members of that club. Are you worth a million dollars—again, not including the equity in your home? It's not an unreasonable question. More than seven million American households today claim total assets of a million dollars or more.

Still, it's probably more likely—more than three and a half times more likely, in fact—that you're among a group we call the mass affluent, people whose total assets add up to anywhere between $100,000 and $1 million. There are 33.4 million mass affluent households in the United States, and chances are pretty good that yours is one of them.

Wealthy Households in America

	MASS AFFLUENT	MILLIONAIRES	MEGA-MILLIONAIRES
	$100K–$1M Net Worth Not Including Primary Residence	$1M–$5M Net Worth Not Including Primary Residence	More than $5M Net Worth Not Including Primary Residence
TOTAL	33,400,000	7,900,000	1,140,000

Do you own a nice home? Do you have a good salary—one commensurate with your skills, training, and responsibilities—or reap a substantial income from your business? Maybe you own a vacation home—or are looking to buy one.

You probably have a 401(k) plan or a portfolio of "buy-and-hold" stocks, bonds, and funds that keep growing with the economy. If so, your total assets very likely add up to at least $100,000, which puts you easily among the mass affluent. That means you qualify, as much as do the rich, the very rich, and the very, very rich, for a new standard of wealth—perpetual wealth for yourself and for the generations of your heirs to come.

WHO ARE AMERICA'S RICH?

A profile of the more than 42 million mass affluent, millionaire, and mega-millionaire American households offers some interesting, even surprising, facts. The wealthiest Americans—our mega-millionaires—tend to be, on average, age sixty-five, or ten years older than those in the mass affluent and millionaire categories. This age difference also accounts for the higher percentage of mega-millionaires who are retired, compared to the 72 percent of mass affluent who are still employed.

Education is another interesting indicator; the data show a direct correlation between wealth and a college degree—notably, that nearly two-thirds of mega-millionaires have advanced degrees. Career choice is also a key driver of wealth. Many so-called "C-level" executives and business owners are mega-millionaires. Professional training also pays: Doctors and lawyers constitute an important segment of the rich in America. In their case, education and career choice have converged—along with the desire, felt by millions of Americans, to get rich and stay rich.

America's Rich

	MASS AFFLUENT	MILLIONAIRES	MEGA-MILLIONAIRES
AVERAGE AGE	54	56	65
EDUCATION	87% College Graduates	91% College Graduates	94% College Graduates
	46% Advanced Degree	57% Advanced Degree	63% Advanced Degree
WORK STATUS	28% Retired	33% Retired	48% Retired
PRIMARY OCCUPATION	8% Senior Corporate Executives	12% Senior Corporate Executives	22% Senior Corporate Executives
	6% Business Owners	6% Business Owners	15% Business Owners
	3% Physician/Dentist	8% Physician/Dentist	10% Physician/Dentist
	16% Other Professional Specialist	10% Other Professional Specialist	9% Other Professional Specialist
	3% Attorney	2% Attorney	7% Attorney
	5% Consultant	3% Consultant	6% Consultant

THE GET-RICH FORMULA

Carnegie, du Pont, Rockefeller. These are names associated with both generous philanthropy and wealth that seems to go on forever—virtual dynasties of wealth. Microsoft's Bill Gates and uberinvestor Warren Buffett will give away well over 90 percent of what they have earned and still have billions to pass down, but of course, they are the wealthiest two people on the planet. You probably won't be able to do quite what these families have managed to do—give away most of their wealth and still have enough to pass down to multiple generations—but by studying the *model* of getting rich, staying rich, and passing it on, as defined by the Rockefellers and the Buffetts—you can create your own prescription for your own version of perpetual wealth.

We've done the studying for you. That's our job, and frankly, the market agrees that we do it better than just about anybody else. What do we study? Each year, we research thousands of wealthy households as well as normal households invested in standard 401(k) and other company plans. By doing the research month after month, we can continually monitor how these people are allocating their assets, the returns they are achieving on their investments, and the approaches they are using in their decision making.

Each year we perform in-depth, mail-based research on approximately 5,000 mass affluent, millionaire, and mega-millionaire households. Again, the aim is to analyze asset allocation and the attitudes and perceptions that go into investment decisions.

We support this in-depth mail research with detailed online research, and we also host focus groups across the country on an ongoing basis to further understand how people get rich and stay rich—and how the shrewdest of these people get rich enough to pass it on.

We issue monthly indices that are carried in all the financial media, including the *Wall Street Journal* and *New York Times*, and we publish subject-specific research reports that are read widely by economists in government, business, and the foundation community. Both of us are often called upon to comment on economic trends or shifts in the market and on changing investment practices. (If you do not recall seeing our faces, there is a chance you may have heard our voices on the radio while listening to the financial news).

Specifically for this book, we conducted in-depth interviews with more than two dozen wealthy individuals who qualify as perpetually wealthy—rich enough to stay rich for their lifetime and to ensure rich lifetimes for multiple future generations. You'll meet many of these folks in the pages that follow, although under different names. We matched what we learned from them against what is known about the great sustainable fortunes of history and about the megafortunes of today's ultrarich. We also looked at the asset allocations of today's garden-variety households—the households of people like you and your neighbors.

We put all this data together and then analyzed what it is you have to do to ensure perpetual wealth. We've found that while there are many ways to get rich, and while there are diverse paths to remaining rich during a single lifetime, there are only two definitive ways to create the kind of wealth that can be bequeathed to multiple generations:

1. **Own income-producing real estate—in addition to your primary residence.** It is thus an asset that earns money for you today and that can be passed down to your heirs as part of your legacy.

2. **Practice what we call continually innovative entrepreneurship**—being involved in or investing and reinvesting in a company, product, or service that represents a whole new way to make money.

Doing both is a surefire way to get rich, stay rich, and pass on your riches to future generations. The great fortunes we have studied all share these two characteristics, whatever the source of the wealth and despite a great diversity of background, geography, educational level, interest, skill, and talent among the progenitors of the fortunes.

It sounds simple, and in a way it is: Involve yourself continually in innovative enterprises, and become an owner of income-producing real estate. Do this and you open the door to getting rich, staying rich, and passing it on to your children, grandchildren, great-grandchildren, and beyond.

But in another way, of course, it is not simple at all. How do you find the innovative enterprise, and how do you immerse yourself in the business? Are you ready for a life-altering career change—ready to become an entrepreneur and take an entrepreneur's risk? If a career change is not in the works, how much money and personal attention should you invest in such enterprises? How do you define "innovative," and how do you ensure that an innovative enterprise will continue to provide a perpetual income stream? As for real estate, which real estate should you buy? When? How? How do you manage your ownership of real estate?

At what point in a career should one start down these paths? How should a business owner allocate funds for investing in or purchasing other businesses? How should the investments or purchases be structured?

In other words, exactly how do you open the door to the kind of wealth we have described? That is precisely the question we'll help you answer in the pages that follow.

BUILD YOUR OWN WEALTH MODEL

Maybe you're a professional—a lawyer, doctor, executive—proud of the accomplishments that are providing you and your family a comfortable living but unaware that you have the means to leave a substantial financial legacy. After all, you reason, the income you make today comes directly from your individual expertise—strenuously obtained through study, effort, and training. But when you go, the expertise goes with you—and the wealth stops streaming, unless you take action while you're very much alive to keep the income flowing for generations.

Perhaps you're a business owner, satisfied that you've built something significant that will provide for a comfortable retirement—but not thinking beyond that. Maybe you inherited a fixed amount of assets or wealth, either through a family member, divorce, or other means. While you are grateful to be on the receiving end of the inheritance, you suspect it is finite; in fact, there are ways to make it expansible. Or maybe you are just now on the brink of attaining wealth, starting up a business venture or beginning a career that will lift you from the ranks of the "well-off" to the more rarefied rank of mass affluent, millionaire, or mega-millionaire.

In any of these cases, you have the power to ensure virtually perpetual wealth for yourself and your heirs. All you really need is to know how to use the same wealth-building tools Carnegie and du Pont and all the other progenitors of sustainable fortunes used. They created the model but they didn't patent it. It's available for your use, and this book is the operating manual.

We'll show you how the model works and how professionals, business owners, corporate managers, trust-fund babies, single women, and others—people you know, people just like you—have used the formula to develop their own individual prescription for creating, keeping, and passing on their money.

Then we'll show you how it can work for you. We'll walk you step by step through the process:

- **A quantitative self-assessment** of your current wealth

- **A qualitative self-assessment** of your positioning vis-à-vis the two keys of perpetual wealth, and

- **An analysis of the gap,** if any, between your current model and the benchmark model established by the perpetually wealthy.

From all this, we'll help you derive your personal prescription—a true action plan for creating your own model of wealth sufficient to pass on and on and on.

But we'll do more than that. In addition to finding the model for getting rich, staying rich, and passing it on, we have, through our research, also uncovered the character traits and mental attitudes that have consistently proved to be decisive factors in attaining such wealth. While character and intellect cannot be taught, the principles, premises, formulas, and standards they drive can be learned. We've learned them, and we'll teach them to you in the chapters that follow.

CHAPTER 1

THE TWO SECRETS OF PERPETUAL WEALTH

Tom Kramer remembers nights when he would sleep in the cab of his pickup truck so he could catch the early snowplow jobs. The truck and the attached plow were the total assets of his fledgling business. His marketing strategy was simple to a fault: drive around his growing Midwestern town asking business owners if they had any work for him to do. Financial control was what his wife, Carol, did at the kitchen table after her teaching job. It meant long days and a lot of sleepless nights for the two of them as they tried to get their small business up and running.

Doug and Laurie Langston started out in a not too dissimilar fashion. Laurie worked to help put Doug through medical school and the long, arduous training in his chosen field, anesthesiology. Laurie was able to be a stay-at-home mom once Doug's suburban East Coast practice began to pay off, which it did (and still does—handsomely). But Doug still puts in long hours and weekends, both because that's what his profession requires and as a hedge against the encroaching pressures of health maintenance and preferred provider plans—HMOs and PPOs.

Sally Brown was widowed in her early fifties, and feels the sting of it every day. She and Jim had married young, headed west, and done everything together, venturing into places and businesses they knew nothing about, taking themselves up the learning curve, parlaying one enterprise into another. Finding herself alone in the world has been a wrench for Sally, and, forced into a new worldview, she is moving ahead slowly and cautiously—one step at a time.

These are three different sets of people from three different parts of the country, with three very different starting places and circumstances. Yet all of them are on their way to creating models of wealth that will make them comfortable for life—a *kind* of wealth that can also ensure such comfort for their heirs for many generations to come.

They're not aware of this. In fact, they're totally oblivious to the fact that they have defined any kind of model at all. Yet Tom and Doug and Sally have all managed to do the two things that will sustain their wealth not just for their lifetimes but for the lifetimes of their heirs and beyond: They have invested in real estate that generates a stream of income and have become involved in innovative enterprises that, in all three cases, fall outside of their primary jobs or endeavors. And although they are not aware of it, being engaged in these two income-producing activities, regardless of whatever else they do with their money, places them in a league with Carnegie and du Pont and Rockefeller. Of course they don't have Rockefeller money, and probably never will. But they share with him and other mega-millionaires the two secrets to making their wealth last well past their lifetimes.

The research is pretty conclusive. From the great ancient fortunes to the old robber barons right up to the new Information Age nabobs, those two secrets—continually innovative entrepreneurship and the ownership of income-producing real estate—make the difference between having money and, for lack of a more economical term, having money forever.

HOW TO SUSTAIN A GREAT FORTUNE—AND HOW NOT TO

It will come as no surprise that the vast majority of the great fortunes made through history can be traced back to a single entrepreneurial individual with vision and imagination, and the confidence to put them to work. But the qualities that create a fortune are not the sorts of things one can pass on to children or grandchildren (other than what is passed on in their genetic code). That is surely one reason why having great wealth is no guarantee of being able to pass it on—certainly not past the first generation to follow. Great fortunes—those counted in the many millions or billions—may sustain succeeding generations out of their sheer size, but history confirms that the amount of money one passes on is not the key determinant in how long the money will last.

The shipping and railroad fortune gained by "Commodore" Cornelius Vanderbilt in the nineteenth century, for example, was one of the greatest in world history. Yet, just 48 years after his death, one of his direct descendants died penniless.

Apparently no one taught Vanderbilt's careless spendthrift heirs how to protect their fortunes.

What happened to this massive amount of money? Was it just frittered away? In a way, yes. But even nonstop spending by a crowd of prodigious consumers would probably not have been enough to liquidate the Vanderbilt fortune as fast as it was dissipated.

The real answer to what happened to all that money lies not in its size, but in how the fortune was structured. Our research shows that the Vanderbilt fortune was not managed in a way that is consistent with our definition of income-producing real estate.

The family's real estate holdings were legendary, including land and buildings in the heart of New York's Manhattan, real estate that would be considered priceless today. But the real estate was repeatedly sold for cash—cash that was repeatedly squandered on such regal distractions as yachting, horse breeding, and auto racing, as well as on the less wholesome pursuits of drugs, alcohol, and divorce settlements. So the steady income those properties could have produced never materialized.

As to involvement in innovative enterprises, there really wasn't any. The family continued to draw its main income from railroads and shipping, both of which were dwindling in importance. (The only real financial innovator among the heirs has been Gloria Vanderbilt, who licensed her artwork and her name for a range of fashion products—and thus created a fortune of her own. But by then, the original Vanderbilt money had been used up.)

It was these two failures that made it possible for the Vanderbilt heirs to sink many millions down the drain.

Another relevant example can be found in the Warburgs, the extraordinary German-Jewish family whose banking riches were gained in Germany in the nineteenth century. Fortunately, the family fortune survived the Nazi regime. Unfortunately, however, those vast sums would not survive the carelessness of succeeding Warburg generations on the American side of the Atlantic.

The managers of the Warburg fortune resolutely stuck to banking and brokerage, often outguessing the market's ups and downs—although not always. In the aristocratic European tradition from which they were raised, they bought art and collectibles rather than real estate. When the younger Warburgs used the fortune more to support their interests in science, philanthropy, and Broadway musicals, the fortune could no longer be sustained.

The Vanderbilt and Warburg failures to endure are thrown into sharper relief by the success of other equally famous fortunes.

Perhaps the classic twentieth-century success story is Sam Walton, founder of today's 6,500 Wal-Mart stores and Sam's Clubs in 15 countries. Walton began his venture into business ownership in 1945 when he purchased a Ben Franklin store in Newport, Arkansas, with help—a loan of $20,000—from his father-in-law. Walton learned the retail trade and established retailing innovations that have since been copied, profiled, and imitated till they are standard operating procedure—namely, fully stocked shelves and longer hours than the competition.

In 1952, Walton opened a new store under the name "Walton Five and Dime." Working with his brother Bud, he kept opening stores throughout the 1950s. By the end of the decade, the Waltons had an "empire" of 16 variety stores in Arkansas and Kansas. However, they were beginning to feel the heat from a new kind of retailer—the new regional discount chains.

To protect his interests and fight off the onslaught of the new breed of competitor, Sam and his wife, Helen, in 1962 put up 95 percent of the money for a new vision of retailing, embodied in the first Wal-Mart store in Rogers, Arkansas. The new vision was an extension of the formula that had worked so well in the Walton Five and Dimes of the 1950s—namely, a recognition that the American consumer was moving away from the traditional general store to a discount variety store with longer hours and a far wider selection of merchandise. Walton stretched the formula to the size of a warehouse; it has grown into the Wal-Mart we know today.

But Walton didn't stop with the reinvention of the local variety store. He also made it a practice to own the real estate under every store whenever possible. And he kept on investing in both the innovation and the real estate. In 1970, Walton took Wal-Mart public, thus providing capital for a massive expansion along both tracks—the retailing innovation and the real estate.

When Walton died in 1992, he left the ownership of his shares to his wife and four children. His son Rob succeeded him as chairman, and the family interests in Wal-Mart were placed in a partnership. Today, the family still owns 39 percent of Sam's vision—a vision that continues to pay well and to refresh the wellhead of wealth that Sam Walton found. As a result, when *Forbes* magazine published its annual list of the world's wealthiest individuals in 2006, remarkably half of the ten top individuals shared the same last name: Walton.

WELLHEADS OF WEALTH

Like the Waltons and other superrich families, today's mega-millionaires derive 43 percent of their income from investments—specifically, from marketable securities and income-producing real estate. This contrasts with mass affluent Americans, whose income from investments is only 20 percent. The mass affluent investor's chief source of income, 57 percent, comes from his/her career/primary job (e.g., earned income). Mega-millionaires, in contrast, derive only 40 percent of their income from their salaries. For you to become one of the megawealthy, you must take steps to ensure your investment income eventually exceeds your salary.

MONEY FOREVER MEANS MONEY NOW

This book is not intended to be an instructor's manual on how to teach your heirs not to fritter away your fortune. Nor is the book's chief aim to suggest that you work feverishly today to enrich heirs in some remote future many decades from now. On the contrary: You're working for you. You're working to get rich and stay rich—and enjoy being rich—*today*.

But here's the kicker, and it may seem counterintuitive: The best way to get really rich *today* is to follow the model for keeping your heirs rich *tomorrow*. That's the fundamental "aha" discovery of our research. That's why Tom Kramer, Doug Langston, and Sally Brown are today enjoying more wealth than they ever dreamed of—because they are following two paths that have the potential to keep their heirs rich forever.

Tom, Doug, and Sally are putting their money to work in other important ways. They're investing some of it in the stock market, socking some of it away for retirement or for their children's college education, spending it on nice homes and vacations and other things that make them happy. But in all three cases, they are using a significant portion of their money to buy real estate properties that produce income, and they are using some of their money to produce new potential income streams from innovative enterprises. The result is that they will make enough money to live rich during their lifetimes, and they will bequeath to their heirs not just vast sums of money, but a model for sustaining perpetual wealth.

AND NOW . . . WHAT DOESN'T WORK

"My business is my golden goose," says Arthur Ellis. "It was my version of investing in the stock market twenty years ago. I take great pride in the business. I came from nothing."

That all sounds well and good, but the problem is that Ellis has only the one golden goose to rely on—and lately, the goose is losing some of its luster. Ellis's golden goose is a jewelry casting business that is highly labor-intensive and whose success rests almost entirely with the Christmas gift-giving season. Recent imports from China have been undercutting the business, and

Ellis is finding it harder and harder to compete. Every July when the "busy season" starts, he blindly doubles his 40-person workforce without any guarantee that the next Christmas will be as lucrative as the one before. In fact, what was once a $20 million business is now a business that does less than $14 million annually.

No wonder Arthur Ellis is stressed out. He has always assumed that the business would support a luxurious retirement and a healthy legacy for his children and grandchildren. Now he is wondering how he will liquidate what is, in Ellis's words, "such a specialty business."

"There are only one or two competitors," Ellis explains, "and they really have no interest in buying my business." Two employees may be interested, but they and Arthur are uncertain that they will get the financing they need.

The fact is that although it's late in the game, Arthur Ellis still has the financial wherewithal to employ the two secrets to having money forever. He is in a good position to recognize innovations in the jewelry technology business, and he could certainly purchase real estate properties to serve as rental units. He has the wherewithal, but he may not have the time. Moreover, Ellis is today so consumed by worry over his one golden goose he is unable to think about alternatives that may deliver more valuable golden eggs in the future.

WHY AND HOW THE MODEL WORKS

Our research also revealed why the model works: It establishes a different kind of criterion for allocating assets and a different way of thinking about investment categories. To be sure, all asset allocation models are aimed at dividing up resources—and spreading risk—in order to meet a particular investment goal. Investors determine whether they are most eager for income, growth, preservation of capital, or some combination thereof. Then, using that goal as the decision-making criterion, they allocate their investments among a range of financial choices: stocks, bonds, mutual funds, investment partnerships, real estate, maybe private equity, and cash or cash equivalents like certificates of deposit or money market funds. The idea is that each of these classes of assets has a different correlation to the others, so if one goes down, another will go up. In any event, that's the way the theory works.

In fact, these traditional asset allocation models typically work perfectly well to achieve the investor's goals. Suppose you are looking to preserve capital toward a particular purpose—the down payment for a house, for example, or a college education. You're not trying to score a big return on your money, and you're not particularly concerned that it multiply in size. In that case, your asset allocation model would be closely linked to the money markets, treasury bonds, and commercial paper—investments promising only a modest gain but posing very little risk to your principal. Then, perhaps working with an advisor, you would divvy up your marketable assets among those investment categories, trying to make sure that there's healthy diversification of credit risk and a maturity strategy that matches your time frame for when you want the funds liquid—that is, available for your use.

And sure enough, within your stated time frame, the model would almost surely achieve your goal: Your capital would be waiting, just a little bit bigger than when you invested it, but absolutely safe and sound.

In contrast, the model of asset allocation for getting rich, staying rich, and passing it on isn't based on theories of correlation or on categories of instruments. It's based on the single, straightforward goal of wealth longevity, and it sets out two paths to that goal.

One path is stability—ensuring a steady stream of income despite the vagaries of the economy and the potential volatility of the financial markets. That's the very definition of real estate. Whatever happens to the economy, people need places to live and work. One way or the other, rent gets paid. By owning real estate, you ensure it gets paid to you.

The other path is renewal—or continually adding to the income stream by identifying fresh income sources, primarily through ongoing reinvestment in innovative enterprises. Each time you do so, you're adding a new way to generate money.

It's essential to take both paths, not just one or the other. Doing both, according to a formula we'll present in the next chapter, achieves an important and tangible synergy that yields something considerably more than the sum of the parts—not just the money represented by a stable income from real estate, and not just the money from investing in innovation. Rather, doing both yields perpetual wealth—enough to have and keep and pass on, which is just what Tom and Doug and Sally are creating, whether they know it or not.

In addition, of course, to their investments in real estate

and continually innovative enterprises, Tom and Doug and Sally are investing other assets in accord with traditional asset allocation models aimed at traditional investment goals. They understand that the model we have presented does not exist in a vacuum, nor does it represent the be-all and end-all of one's financial lives. Rather, it should be viewed as a supplement to traditional investing, not a replacement for it.

A PORTRAIT IN PERPETUAL WEALTH: AN ORDINARY GUY

He's nowhere near being a millionaire. Not yet, anyway. Rather, he's a midlevel manager at a small Midwestern company who makes a midlevel salary and lives an unremarkable midlevel lifestyle. Yet Mark Prentice is well on his way to achieving the kind of wealth that lasts virtually forever. An entrepreneurial curiosity propels him to action time and again, while he also maintains an unswerving commitment to successful real estate investing. These are the key ingredients, and Mark puts them to work just about every which way he can.

On a salary commensurate with his growing responsibilities, Mark is able to support his wife and two kids in a new house in a pleasant suburb outside Chicago. His commute requires just about an hour of train time each way—time that Mark invariably spends on his laptop. He is young enough to be an Internet guy but seasoned enough to understand the Web's real money-making potential.

Mostly, Mark has made use of his familiarity with eBay to turn some quick, profitable deals—both on and off the World Wide Web.

Perhaps his most creative venture was his foray into the shoe resale business. Learning via the Web of a warehouse full of mostly athletic shoes available for sale, Mark bought the lot at a phenomenally low price of $7.50 per pair. He marketed them on eBay—some were brand-name items—and sold the entire supply at an average price of $22 per pair, plus the cost of shipping. Mark made enough on this single resale deal for a down payment on an apartment building.

And that was precisely his next move. He put down 25 percent of the building's purchase price and mortgaged the rest. The rent covers his monthly payments, while the real benefits are the depreciation and tax breaks he receives, as well as the equity in the building—which is growing with every passing month.

Because he owns only one building and is good with his hands, Mark is able to do most of the maintenance himself. He does it well; he is a handy guy who can fix things efficiently and cost-effectively. For example, when he recently bought a new home for his family, he did so even though it badly needed a new kitchen. Surfing eBay, Mark found a set of high-end kitchen cabinets and granite countertops for sale—the contractor hadn't measured right, and the pieces simply didn't fit in a rehab. Mark picked up these items on the cheap and installed them in his kitchen over a long, exhausting weekend. Total cost? About 10 percent of what he would have paid in the retail market.

Yes, Mark is sometimes frustrated by annoying late night calls from tenants with trivial problems, but reminds himself this is an important first step that will secure a lifetime of wealth for himself and his family, not to mention generations to come.

Mark continues to maintain his day job at the company. He likes the work, is good at it, and looks upon his position as an anchor of security. But on the train and on weekends, he continues to surf the Net and scan eBay for innovative, money-making opportunities. As of this writing, he was looking into baseball cards, but he had an idea for a whole new approach to marketing them. . . .

CHAPTER 2

WHAT SEPARATES THE PERPETUALLY WEALTHY FROM EVERYONE ELSE

At sixty-two, Mike Lester is as entrepreneurial as he was when he was twenty-two. He has a penchant for the new, a flair for the start-up venture, an innate savvy about the market. That's just the kind of guy he is; it's his character, his personality. That character has driven Mike to attain a level of wealth that means he never has to worry about money again. It has also prompted him to create a model of wealth that will sustain his heirs for generations to come. In this chapter, you'll get a close look at the model that has led to Mike's extraordinary financial success. In fact, it is such a perfect example that it can be considered the prototype for perpetual wealth.

Of course, Mike didn't set out to exemplify a model. He didn't set out to create perpetual wealth. As you'll understand when you read his story, all he really wanted to do was scratch out some sort of living. His actual achievements far exceeded anything he had imagined.

In fact, until we told him, Mike had absolutely no idea that he was the poster boy for the kind of wealth we describe in this book. When we told him how well he was doing, we were surprised by his reaction: He just shrugged. Like so many of the people in this book who have created their own personal wealth models, Mike had intuited the way—simply by doing what came naturally and what seemed right.

One cannot achieve Mike's kind of wealth by trying to imitate his personality. The totality of his temperament, abilities, weaknesses, quirks, qualities, and talents is absolutely particular to him and influenced the many moves and many decisions he made in his career. Just about all of these moves helped make him wealthy enough to qualify as perpetually wealthy. The best one can do is to extract from Mike's story a few key building blocks that can be used to erect one's own specific model of perpetual wealth.

We've changed the names and a few details, but here is Mike's story.

Mike went right to work after graduating from high school (which his mother insisted he do). He worked full time at the job he had held after school and summers: assistant buyer—a glorified stock boy—in New York's garment industry. He kept his eyes and ears open, took a few night-school courses in business and accounting, and at the age of twenty-two borrowed enough money to take over a small and moribund fabric shop in a commercial building on the edge of the garment district.

By focusing on high-end woven designs, he was eventually able to parlay the small shop into a fabric empire. He sold the company when he was thirty but then shrewdly bought the building it was housed in and immediately opened his second business one flight up: a style and color trend forecasting service for the fashion industry.

Mike also bought more real estate nearby, content to wait for the inevitable day—which came within a few years—when the grungy garment-district neighborhood would turn trendy and chic. He bought country properties as well, starting with a weekend house in Connecticut before expanding his holdings to include commercial properties and other residences in Connecticut, upstate New York, and in neighboring New Jersey. By the time he opened his third business, a computer-assisted fabric and color design service, Mike Lester had created a virtually fail-safe model of perpetual wealth.

In a final flourish, Mike brought it all home by involving his children. Daughter Erica manages the family's real estate holdings while son Peter runs the fashion-related activities. The three meet frequently, along with their spouses, to brainstorm ideas for new enterprises and discuss investment possibilities. They have no desire to sit on their hands and simply count their father's money. The younger Lesters *want* to be involved—in an ongoing, hands-on way—in refreshing and enhancing the fortune they've been given.

Meanwhile, Mike hasn't stopped leveraging the model he instinctively created. His latest interest is wireless communication, and as of this writing, he has been exploring ways to create a new business model in the networking industry, which will almost assuredly become his fourth successful foray into the business start-up world.

A PERFECT 10

The bottom line is that, as a model of how to get rich, stay rich, and pass it on, Mike Lester is that rare thing in life—a perfect 10. What makes him a 10? First of all, he is the unwitting exemplar of the two essentials of continuous wealth: repeated and consistent investment in innovative enterprises and creative management of income-producing real estate.

ANATOMY OF A PERFECT 10

In Mike Lester's case, the two keys to his stunning financial success—which led to perpetual wealth—lay in his intense focus on the activities that became his passions. It's safe to say that Mike was more impassioned about innovation than about fashion, more interested in the rents than in the renters. So it's not surprising that he "performed" so well in both those activities, as the ratings chart on page 29 makes clear.

But perhaps even more important, Mike's total portfolio is an exact match of the benchmark model for getting rich enough to stay rich and pass it on to future generations. This benchmark is a simple investment model that represents the categories into which the perpetually wealthy divide their resources, and how much of their resources they allocate to each category.

We base the model on our examination of sustainable fortunes from history and the present day, on our in-depth interviews with families throughout the country, and on our annual

JUST ABOUT A PERFECT 10	
How well engaged in continually innovative enterprises	**RATING: 10** • Built, then sold initial business • Started a second business • Even today is investing in a new business (wireless communications)
How well invested in income-producing real estate	**RATING: 10** • Bought properties in "industrial" district where space is at a premium • Continues to invest in properties
Likelihood of achieving perpetual wealth	**RATING: 9–10** • Is on the right course, especially since he is including family members in the business—but subtract a single point to allow for the uncertainties of the financial markets
For how many generations?	**GENERATIONS: 3-4** • Garment district real estate will continue to be lucrative for many generations • A model of family involvement has been created to keep spirit of entrepreneurship alive

research into the financial habits and practices of more than 5,000 households that have the potential to become perpetually wealthy. Mike Lester divvied up his wealth just the way the progenitors of the perpetual-wealth fortunes divvy up theirs—asset class by asset class. His asset allocation model is a perfect 10 because it exactly matches the asset allocation that is the benchmark model of wealth that lasts and lasts and lasts, continually renewing itself, virtually forever.

THE BENCHMARK MODEL FOR PERPETUAL WEALTH

The accompanying chart shows what the model looks like.

Get Rich, Stay Rich, Pass It On: The Benchmark

INVESTMENTS	PERCENTAGE OF TOTAL HOUSEHOLD ASSETS
MARKETABLE SECURITIES...35–45	
• Cash and short-term securities...............................5–7	
• Stocks, bonds, and mutual funds 30–40	
• Alternatives, including hedge funds, venture capital, private equity 4–5	
• Other investment products, including unit investment trusts, 529s, and the like 3–4	
PRIVATELY HELD BUSINESSES (CONTINUALLY INNOVATIVE ENTERPRISES)..................25–35	
REAL ESTATE 23–29	
• Equity in principal residence..................................11–13	
• Income-producing property..................................3–6	
• Second home 5–7	
• Other real estate 3–5	
• Undeveloped land..2–4	
• Third/additional residences 2–4	
LIFE INSURANCE AND ANNUITIES 5–7	
RETIREMENT PLAN...3–5	
OTHER INVESTMENTS 3–5	

It shows how investment assets are allocated by those who have achieved or are on their way to achieving perpetual wealth. By "investments," we mean items of economic value that you own and that can be sold for cash, if needed, but that have been purchased for the sole aim of capital appreciation (like shares of stock that you bought because you feel it will increase in value in the future).

There are different classes of these investment assets. Many are financial instruments—stocks, bonds, money market accounts, annuities—but real estate is also a key investment, especially if you are seeking to pass on your wealth forever. In the benchmark model of getting rich, staying rich, and passing it on, that includes your primary residence; yes, it's your home, but it's an investment as well.

Investment experts preach the wisdom of allocating investment assets among different asset classes as a way to spread the risk. In other words, don't put all your eggs in one basket. Instead, put a few eggs in the stock market basket, a few in the bonds basket, a few in a readily accessible money market account, and a few in real estate investments.

That way, if the stock market tanks, you may still profit from the assets you've put into bonds, the money market, and real estate. In fact, many of these investments tend to have a negative correlation with one another: As one increases, the other decreases. Typically, when the value of stocks goes up, the value of bonds goes down. So asset allocation makes sense for many reasons, and the need to spread the risk certainly plays a role in the asset allocation model of the perpetually wealthy.

Our model supports the traditional asset allocation discipline but emphasizes a far greater investment in real estate and privately held businesses. Income-producing real estate and privately held businesses can be passed on to your heirs with little difficulty. More important, your children, grandchildren, nieces, or nephews will be far more inclined to hold onto the real estate and enjoy the monthly income, particularly when that is compared to traditional stocks and bond investments, which are more liquid and easier to sell. Your heirs may also take an active interest in the management of the business and encourage other family members to do the same.

WHAT ARE THE WEALTHY INVESTED IN?

Where, exactly, do mega-millionaires put their money? Which investment products do they choose when they go into the capital market? And how much do they invest in each type of product?

Just below half, 40 to 45 percent, of the typical mega-millionaire portfolio is invested in marketable assets—stocks, bonds, mutual funds, and other securities. This percentage varies slightly from year to year due to market fluctuations. Those are relatively liquid assets—that is, they're pretty readily convertible into cash. The rest of the assets in the mega-millionaire portfolio, however, are not so liquid. They include the principal residence, which typically averages 12 percent of the total portfolio; investment real estate, which also averages about 12 percent; privately held businesses, which account for 25–35 percent; and insurance, annuities, and retirement accounts, which in aggregate average approximately 10 percent of the total.

Here's how mega-millionaire households allocate the 40 to 45 percent of their assets that are invested in marketable assets. They are heavily invested in individual stocks (22 percent) and individual bonds (14 percent). In fact, the richer they are, the more they invest in these standard capital market investments. The average mega-millionaire balance in these two investment categories together is over $4.6 million.

Mega-millionaires also invest in standard mutual funds, as do millions of non-mega-millionaire Americans. In fact, mutual funds represent one of the most common investments regardless of level of wealth—possibly because they are perceived by investors as being one of the safest, least risky investments.

The average balance invested in United States stock mutual funds by mega-millionaires is $1 million, along with an average of a half-million dollars in municipal bond mutual funds. Investing outside the United States is also on the mega-millionaire's radar screen, with an average of $400,000 invested in international mutual funds. Exchange Traded Funds (ETFs), a newer investment product, is also popular with mega-millionaires, who have invested on average over $300,000 in these funds.

Unlike mutual funds, or even stocks and bonds, alternative investments are something most of us don't typically invest in. Venture capital, hedge funds, private equity, and private placements are pretty much within the exclusive purview of the very wealthy. Given the complex nature of these investments, the Securities and Exchange Commission has established requirements that investors must meet to purchase alternative securities. One is deemed to be an "accredited investor" if individual net worth or joint net worth with a spouse exceeds $1 million or income exceeds $200,000 ($300,000 jointly with spouse) in each of the previous two years with the expectation of the same level of income in the current year. Clearly, the mega-millionaire is deemed to be accredited, having invested over $650,000 in private equities, $300,000 in venture capital, and $730,000 in hedge funds.

Like most Americans, mega-millionaires are saving for retirement in retirement plans. In fact, they are invested in virtually the full range of plans available—from rollover Individual Retirement Accounts (IRAs) to 401(k) plans. What is particularly interesting is that the wealthiest of the mega-millionaires—those with net worth exceeding $25 million—have over $2 million in IRAs and over $900,000 in Roth IRAs.

What does this pattern of investment tell us about getting rich, staying rich, and passing it on? It tells us that those who have done so are well diversified in their investments. It suggests to us that they are not overly cautious in investing—although that is, of course, a subjective judgment, since mega-millionaires have more money to put at risk.

It also confirms the earning power of a combination of investments in real estate and in privately held businesses. In terms of both percentage of allocation and the total dollars allocated, the dual investment in real estate and innovative entrepreneurship is distinctive. It confirms that these are the two secrets to achieving the extreme level of wealth we describe at length throughout the book.

A MATTER OF PROPORTION

The essential lesson of the benchmark model for perpetual wealth is not that it ensures diversification of risk—that's a given—but rather that it outlines the most beneficial proportions in which the marketable assets are allocated. Our research makes this absolutely clear: In the benchmark model, fully half of all investment assets are allocated to the two asset classes that distinguish sustainable fortunes: privately held businesses and real estate. In fact, households that have achieved—or are on their way to—perpetual wealth typically invest at least 50 percent and as much as 68 percent of their investment assets in private enterprises and real estate.

Certainly, the character of those private enterprises (they must be continually innovative) and of the real estate (it must produce income) you invest in is equally important. But our interest here is in the percentage of the allocations to these two investment activities, for that is an essential distinguishing mark of having money forever, as example after example makes absolutely clear.

Of equal interest is how the percentages break out between and within the two key asset classes. Take a look.

PRIVATELY HELD—AND CONTINUALLY INNOVATIVE—BUSINESSES

Note that the households rich enough to stay rich and pass it on invest just a bit more in private enterprises than in real estate. This emphasis on privately held—and, preferably, innovative—enterprises is a key distinction between the perpetually wealthy and the "merely" wealthy. In fact, our research makes it clear that income from an ongoing business in which the individual is personally involved represents the largest percentage of the total income of those who have achieved the status of the megawealthy.

This makes perfect sense. Think about it: Today's inheritors of great fortunes are the beneficiaries of the innovations in which their "ancestors" were involved one, two, or three generations ago. The Model T was a startling innovation for its time; it is certainly still paying off for the Ford heirs today. And what about the grandchildren of the folks who in the 1950s bought stock in a company that manufactured punch card tabulating machines—because they suspected the company's new "defense calculator" might go places? Those grandchildren are still getting dividends from their shares in IBM.

These companies are now "publicly traded," enabling anyone (with available funds to become an owner by purchasing shares of the stock) to benefit from the expected profits. In contrast, our model stresses the *creation* of innovative companies, products, services, etc. Ford was founded in 1903 and remained a private company until it became a publicly traded company in 1956. Certainly a great deal of wealth was created by the Ford Motor Company, and the Ford family's wealth was increased exponentially when shares of the company were sold to the public in 1956. Similarly, IBM was founded in 1889 by Herman Hollerith and went public in 1916.

However, thousands of innovative privately held companies never go public. Ownership remains in the hands of the founders, who manage the company year in and year out while searching for the next game-changing innovative product or service. Many family members of owners of privately owned companies are exposed to the family business early in life at a time when they have the choice of becoming involved in that business. Whether family members immerse themselves in the day-to-day operations or not, the ownership of the business can be passed on to multiple generations who will benefit from the profits and enhanced value of the enterprise.

There's something else about involvement in privately held

enterprises: it diversifies one's portfolio beyond financial instruments like stocks and bonds and even beyond real estate into something that provides goods and services. Such enterprises feed the overall economy—we are all consumers of goods and services, after all—so they are, in a sense, an assurance of economic activity in the future. It's good to be a stakeholder in such activity.

As we'll explain in more detail in Chapter 5, there are many ways to become involved in continually innovative enterprises. Whichever path you choose, the involvement represents a bet on the future that is a distinct feature of the prototype benchmark model for getting rich, staying rich, and passing it on.

REAL ESTATE

Real estate occupies a substantive proportion of the benchmark perpetual wealth model—some 23 percent to 29 percent. In fact, we have found that for those on their way to perpetual wealth, investing in real estate is a key objective, while for those already there, it is an acknowledged must-have in their well-constructed portfolio.

How do the perpetually wealthy get involved in real estate? And how deep is their commitment to this key portfolio holding? As our research makes clear, they are deeply involved—in terms of the numbers of them who have invested in real estate, the raw dollar amounts they have invested, and the range and types of real estate properties they own and manage.

Among mega-millionaires, 75 percent own investment real

estate, and this already impressive number increases from there, 88 percent of those families with a net worth of $25 million or more own investment real estate of one type or another.

We have also studied the real estate investment behaviors of mega-millionaires based on their career choices. Business owners and senior corporate executives are focused on investment real estate, 80 percent of those who own their own businesses have investment property in their portfolios, while 70 percent of senior corporate executives own investment real estate.

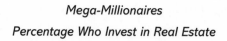

Mega-Millionaires
Percentage Who Invest in Real Estate

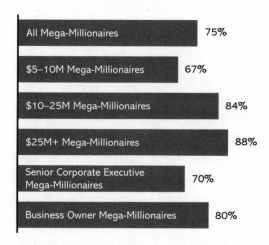

All of these figures paint an even clearer picture when we examine the average market values of the properties in which mega-millionaires are invested. The average mega-millionaire household owns almost $3 million in investment properties, and the very wealthiest household owns properties worth an average of over $7 million.

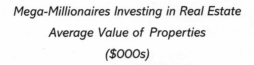

What are these properties? Other than primary residence, the mega-millionaire preference is for a second home, as 48 percent of them own a favorite getaway or weekend residence with an average market value of over $1.2 million.

Otherwise, mega-millionaires' investment real estate consists of rental property with an average market value of $2.5 million, undeveloped land with an average market value of $1.1 million, and other investment properties such as commercial properties.

Over the past 25 years, a new category of real estate investment has come to the fore: time-shares and vacation clubs. In time-shares, investors buy "privileges" to use a housing unit—condo, townhouse, or even a stand-alone home—for a specific period of time each year at specific destination locations. In a vacation club, the investor buys an interest in a partnership or corporation that owns individual homes in typically desirable locations—the Caribbean, Vail, London, New York, etc.

Shareowners are basically buying the right to use the properties for one or two months a year.

Investments in time-shares and vacation clubs generally have a minimum investment of $100,000 to $500,000. Interestingly, the wealthiest mega-millionaires have significantly higher investment levels in these real estate categories.

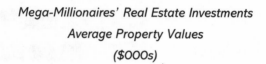

Mega-Millionaires' Real Estate Investments
Average Property Values
($000s)

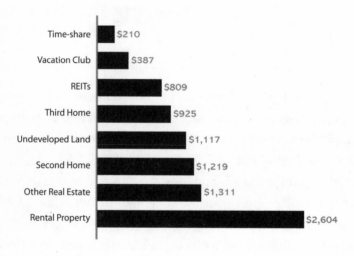

Time-share	$210
Vacation Club	$387
REITs	$809
Third Home	$925
Undeveloped Land	$1,117
Second Home	$1,219
Other Real Estate	$1,311
Rental Property	$2,604

Why are the wealthy so profoundly and pervasively invested in real estate? One reason may be that real estate seems an easy place to start acquiring assets. After all, everybody lives somewhere, so buying a residence as an investment not only makes sense, it seems familiar; it's something people feel competent doing. And of course, given the income tax savings, buying makes a good deal more economic sense than renting.

Business owners, to be sure, are more likely to invest in commercial property with which they are familiar, than in residences, while many professionals (doctors, lawyers) "split the difference"—they often buy into commercial real estate after they have purchased a starter residential rental income property.

Our research shows that once people dive into the real estate investing market, they stay involved across the board and at just about every possible level of the wealth spectrum. Rental properties are the most popular form of real estate investment. Mega-millionaires own rental properties with an average value of just under $3 million, while far less wealthy households, those just starting out in real estate investing, acquire properties valued at anywhere from $100,000 to $500,000.

As the value of these starter properties rises, owners parlay that value into the purchase of properties of increasing value—typically, by borrowing against the appreciation of the starter property to get the down payment for the next property. Moreover, as the wealth of these investors rises in general, the number of them that invest in more real estate also grows.

And the ways of investing in real estate are as varied as the people doing the investing.

One couple—a New Jersey contractor and his wife (we'll call them Bob and Betty)—bought an apartment building at the birth of each of their four children. It was tough going with the first two kids, as Bob and Betty "scraped together the money," in Betty's words, for a couple of marginal properties. But they were then able to leverage those properties to buy the third and fourth apartment buildings for children numbers three and four. As each child grew to college age, Bob and

Betty assessed the market as a prelude to a key decision on each building. If the market was on the upswing, they sold the building to finance the child's education. If the market was steady or in a downturn, they used the building's income to pay tuition and fees. It was a surefire plan for ensuring that all four children received high-quality educations.

A grandfather we'll call Ted had a similar idea—but with a slightly different twist. Having bought buildings throughout his lifetime, much like Mike Lester, Ted made each building the center of separate trusts he set up for each of his grand-children. As each turned twenty-five, it was up to him or her to decide whether to maintain the building to continue to reap its income or to sell it to realize a quick gain either for further in-vestment or for some other purpose (with Grandpa asking no questions and offering no advice).

Homes and stores and office buildings are not the only in-vestment real estate choices, however. Undeveloped land is a common investment—probably because it is often an easier "starter" purchase than developed property. It can also, how-ever, be a more risky proposition. Although it is logical to sup-pose that housing or commercial needs may one day make it necessary to build on a piece of undeveloped property, its fu-ture use is, by definition, speculative at the time of purchase. In fact, it will have an initial negative impact on cash flow due to the real estate taxes and insurance that will be required to maintain the property.

Real estate investment trusts—REITs—are another path to investing in real estate. Most REITs are bought and sold like stock on the major exchanges. They invest in real estate either by buying properties and receiving rental income or by invest-ing in mortgages and receiving interest on the mortgage loans.

Either way, the trusts enable investors to earn income from real estate and diversify their investment portfolios.

We've also found that whatever the form of the real estate investment, the perpetually wealthy view real estate as a long-term investment, not a get-rich-quick gimmick. Perhaps for that reason virtually all households and business owners rely on third-party professionals—real estate agents, lawyers, and accountants—for help in obtaining the right property in the right market, for understanding tax issues, and for handling the paperwork and ensuring compliance with all laws and required procedures. Clearly, they regard these investments with great seriousness of purpose, and they want the best expert advice and assistance they can get.

NONKEY ASSETS

With the two secrets to perpetual wealth—real estate investments and innovative private businesses—accounting for at least half of the assets in our benchmark model, to what other asset classes are resources typically allocated? Our research shows that in the benchmark model, remaining assets are typically divvied up among:

- marketable securities

- life insurance and annuities

- retirement plans

- "other" investments

Marketable securities—easily converted into cash if needed—in fact make up the bulk of the model. Life insurance, annuities, and retirement plans all serve as savings mechanisms. "Other" investments might include fine arts and collectibles, foreign currencies, perhaps precious metals, and the like.

All these traditional investments are standard elements in any classic investment portfolio. Some or all are no doubt in your portfolio or in your 401(k) or IRA account. The difference, however, between the classic portfolio and our benchmark model of getting rich, staying rich, and passing it on, is that in the latter, these traditional investments make up 50 percent or less of the total portfolio, with the other 50 percent or more dedicated to the two secrets of perpetual wealth.

How can you begin to allocate your own assets to create your personal model of money forever? That's the next step in the process.

CHAPTER 3

ASSESSING YOUR
CURRENT WEALTH STATUS

The first step toward gaining a level of wealth that continues to nourish future generations is to know how far you need to go to get there. That's what this chapter is about.

You'll kick it off by determining exactly where you're starting from. You'll profile the allocation of your assets today and then measure the difference between that allocation and the benchmark model of perpetual wealth—especially in terms of the two key components for getting rich, staying rich, and passing it on.

The result? You will have dimensioned the *financial* difference between where you stand today and the benchmark model of the perpetually wealthy. That will give you a quantitative context for creating your own personal wealth model—and not just any model, but the model we have extensively described in the first chapters of this book.

YOUR INVESTMENT ASSETS TODAY

On page 47 is the template of the benchmark model—without the numbers filled in. They're for you to complete—as you measure your current wealth and indicate how it's allocated. Note that we've marked in bold the two investment areas of greatest interest, highest importance, and sharpest focus in terms of getting rich, staying rich, and passing it on—namely, privately held businesses and real estate. That's so you can pay particular attention to those numbers—if any—as you write them down. Keep them highlighted, and hold the thought.

Start by totaling up the dollar value of each of your investment activity assets. It's a less formidable task than you think. Yes, you'll probably have to dig around for various statements and documents—unless you're an extremely organized person who has everything carefully filed and tagged—and you may have to make some phone calls or do some online surfing. But all the numbers the template asks you for are available, and it's important that you fill them in accurately.

Suppose you work for a corporation. Your compensation consists of your salary, which is not an issue here; most likely a health insurance plan, also not an issue; and a qualified defined contribution retirement plan—probably a 401(k). Of these three components of your compensation package, your retirement plan is the one that qualifies as an investment asset, so write the value of it in the retirement box. If you don't know the value of your 401(k) offhand (and you're likely not to), you can almost surely find it online, via phone, or on your PDA; all you need is your account number and possibly an online password. If you've forgotten the account number and don't have a

Get Rich, Stay Rich, Pass It On:
Where You Stand Today

INVESTMENTS	DOLLAR VALUE	PERCENTAGE OF YOUR HOUSEHOLD'S TOTAL ASSETS
MARKETABLE SECURITIES • Cash and short-term securities • Stocks, bonds, and mutual funds • Alternatives, including hedge funds, venture capital, private equity • Other investment products, including unit investment trusts, etc.		
PRIVATELY HELD BUSINESSES (CONTINUALLY INNOVATIVE ENTERPRISES)		
REAL ESTATE • **Principal residence** • **Income-producing property** • **Second home** • **Other real estate** • **Undeveloped land** • **Third/additional residences**		
LIFE INSURANCE AND ANNUITIES		
RETIREMENT PLAN		
OTHER INVESTMENTS		
TOTAL		

statement handy, check with your company's human resources department.

If instead of a 401(k) retirement plan you have a defined benefit or pension plan, check with your human resources department to determine your vested balance—that is, the amount of the payment that should be available to you when you leave your job. This will typically be available as a lump sum distribution or a pension payment available after age fifty-five.

If you plan to take the lump sum distribution—a single payment that you would most probably roll into an IRA and invest as you or your advisor deem appropriate—write this value in the Retirement Plan category. If you choose instead to receive a monthly retirement check—or have the amount automatically deposited into your checking account—this is considered monthly income, even if it becomes a spouse benefit after your death. Do not add the value of this pension to the retirement plan field on the model. Of course, if you are fortunate enough to have a supplemental or nonqualified retirement benefit, add the vested value to the Retirement Plan field.

Chances are good that you have an Individual Retirement Account. Depending on when you opened the account, it may be a pretax, posttax, or Roth IRA. Check your latest statement, and write the value of that account in the Retirement Plan field as well.

We'll also assume that you're in the financial market on an individual basis—and have been ever since your grandfather had the good sense to buy you some IBM or Microsoft stock as a graduation gift from high school. When you graduated from college, other family members gave you bonds. As soon as you started your first job, you invested in a mutual fund. Shortly after the birth of your first child, you transferred some of these investments to a 529 college savings plan, and you've added 529s for each additional child.

What's more, after your last bonus, your financial advisor

talked you into investing in a bond unit trust—and you're pleased she did so. All of these constitute marketable securities—stocks, bonds, a range of investment products—and all have a dollar value. Check your statements for each, or call your broker, and write down the dollar value in the appropriate fields.

Parenthood also prompted you to take out a life insurance policy. If you have absolutely no idea where you put the statement sent to you by the insurance company—and this is likely to be a once-a-year statement—call your insurance agent to get the latest figure for the cash value of your policy. Be very clear that *cash* value is what you're interested in, *not* the *face* value of your insurance; the difference is important. Write down the cash value number in the Life Insurance and Annuities field.

THE TWO SECRETS: WHERE DO YOU STAND?

You own your own home, and since its value has risen steadily since you purchased it, your equity in the home is substantial. Perhaps you own a second home as well—nothing fancy, just a rustic little cabin in the mountains you love to escape to on weekends. The county in which your cabin is located is a fairly marginal area economically, but village revitalization is all the rage right now. Sensing that the market will only get hotter, you and your spouse have bought a small storefront on Main Street that the church thrift shop recently moved into. For the moment, the property is producing a steady, if small, rental income. You're even thinking it might make sense to buy another storefront, start your own little business, hire a local to manage it, and see how it plays out.

This scenario is so commonplace that if it doesn't describe you or someone you know, it probably comes pretty close. Is it a starting point for getting rich, staying rich, and passing it on? Fill in the Real Estate fields of the model and find out.

You may currently own your own business outright or with a few partners. Millions do. These companies range from dry cleaners to restaurants to manufacturing firms to service companies. They come in all shapes and sizes, and they are the backbone of the American economy. More important, each one has a value, and it's important to measure and note the value of your business in determining where you stand on your journey to perpetual wealth.

What does valuing a business consist of? At the end of the day, a business is worth what someone else will pay you for it should you decide to sell. A business valuation exercise estimates that "price." It will likely start with an analysis of your customers—particularly the people who are repeat customers. This universe represents your income stream and is a good starting point for valuing your business.

But to properly value a business, you will probably want to get expert assistance. If you do so regularly and already know the objective valuation of your business, enter this value in the Privately Held Businesses field. If you have not valued your business in the past few years, this is a good time to do so. While there are plenty of firms out there that do nothing but business valuations, we suggest you start with your tax accountant. As the professional most familiar with your business operations, not to mention traditional valuation models (e.g., discounted cash-flow models), he or she is in a strong position to value the business or to refer you to an advisor who can.

If you are a partner in a professional firm—a law firm, consulting firm, or physician's practice—your interest has value and should be included in this category as well. But suppose you're an investor in a private enterprise rather than the owner or the individual who manages the day-to-day operations. Perhaps it's a friend's business, or maybe you're a member of a partnership shared with family members. Whatever the precise nature of the investment, this business has a value; your percentage interest of that value should be indicated in the field for Privately Held Businesses.

Interested in the value of the businesses privately held by America's wealthy? There is a significant difference in the average value of a privately held business compared to the value of a professional practice. The privately held businesses owned by mega-millionaires are valued at over $5.5 million, compared to the average value of professional practices of $3.1 million. The privately held business can be passed on to multiple generations while the professional practice cannot since the doctor or lawyer is the key "asset" of the firm.

Privately Held Business and
Professional Practice Market Values
($000s)

Once you've totaled up the dollar value of all your assets, break down the allocations by percentage, and write in those figures in the appropriate column.

You're now looking at a comprehensive picture of your wealth today, highlighting exactly where you stand on the two secrets to getting rich, staying rich, and passing it on.

CALCULATING THE DIFFERENCE

Now, compare your percentage allocation model against the benchmark model of having money forever by completing the chart provided here.

INVESTMENTS	BENCHMARK PERCENTAGE OF TOTAL HOUSEHOLD ASSETS	MY PERCENTAGE OF TOTAL HOUSEHOLD ASSETS
MARKETABLE SECURITIES	35–45	
• Cash and short-term securities	5–7	
• Stocks, bonds, and mutual funds	30–40	
• Alternatives, including hedge funds, venture capital, private equity	4–5	
• Other investment products, including unit investment trusts, 529s, and the like	3–4	
PRIVATELY HELD BUSINESSES (CONTINUALLY INNOVATIVE ENTERPRISES)	25–35	
REAL ESTATE	23–29	
• **Equity in principal residence**	11–13	
• **Income-producing property**	3–6	
• **Second home**	5–7	
• **Other real estate**	3–5	
• **Undeveloped land**	2–4	
• **Third/additional residences**	2–4	
LIFE INSURANCE AND ANNUITIES	5–7	
RETIREMENT PLAN	3–5	
OTHER INVESTMENTS	3–5	

The result? You've calculated the financial difference between your investments today and your future investment activities to help you understand exactly what you need to do to achieve perpetual wealth. Using the worksheets we've provided, you can see just where and how far you have to go in allocating or reallocating investments to create your own personal model of perpetual wealth.

For example, the benchmark holds that privately held businesses should comprise between 25 to 35 percent of your total assets. How does your current profile measure up? Real estate should make up 23 to 29 percent. If your only real estate holding is your primary residence, you have a fair distance to go to begin to build your own model of perpetual wealth.

Does this mean you should immediately sell some of your stocks from your diversified portfolio of marketable securities and buy a rental property? Or cash in your life insurance policy and invest in a privately held business? *No.* Absolutely not. The truth is that strictly quantitative allocation is not the whole story, and creating perpetual wealth isn't a zero-sum game in which you simply shift assets from one investment class to another.

Rather, there is a qualitative heft to the privately held businesses that will comprise 25 percent to 35 percent of your wealth model. They should be the kind of continually innovative enterprises we've defined earlier, and they should be businesses in which you are personally engaged. Simply buying one or more privately held businesses to fulfill the aforementioned 25 to 35 percent allocation will not lead to perpetual wealth; it will lead only to a rearrangement of your assets.

Similarly, owning enough homes to achieve the 23 to 29 percent real estate ratio of the model may provide you with many bedrooms in which to sleep, but it won't contribute to your getting rich, staying rich, and passing it on. For that, your real estate holdings will need to alternate between personal residences and income-producing properties, and the latter should represent a wide variety of options.

The bottom line is this: Simply chasing the perpetual wealth model we have described by buying up one-off businesses or a handful of real estate properties simply will not work. It may very well be a prescription for failure. The key to success lies in your ability to personalize the elements of the model and make them your own. Ultimately, our model must become *your* model, written in your own hand with only your fingerprints discernable. Otherwise, you stand very little chance of achieving the kind of wealth we have described.

Think of the difference between where you are now and where you need to be as a compass setting; it's a bearing that will show you where to go, but in order to get there you must set your own course based on your own circumstances, objectives, personality, and, of course, on what "feels right" to you.

Figuring out your individual feel-right point is the next step in the process.

A PORTRAIT IN PERPETUAL WEALTH: THE CONSUMMATE PROFESSIONAL

Like most professionals, Doug Langston, M.D., paid his dues for his comfortable lifestyle. Although he received a full scholarship to a local university for his undergraduate education, he financed four years of medical school with student loans, while his wife, Laurie, a teacher, served as the family breadwinner. But even Laurie's job and a small stipend were not quite enough to subsidize the needs of their growing family during Doug's internship and two plum residencies in anesthesiology. The result? Before he ever earned a penny as a highly trained medical specialist, Doug Langston was deeply in debt.

It meant that in the early years of his earning power, most of his assets were perforce allocated to debt repayment. Still, Doug and Laurie made sure to establish college saving plans for their three children the minute each was born so the kids wouldn't have to go into debt for their educations the way their father did. (The Langstons converted these into 529 college savings plans after Congress authorized such plans in 1996.)

The older children are out of the house now—one in law school, one in the military—and the Langstons' "baby" will enter college next year. Although Doug's earning power is formidable and continues to grow, there's been little letup in his work schedule; he is typically on call most weekends, lectures around the country, and rarely takes a vacation. Mostly, this is because Doug sees his profession as a calling as much as a means of employment, but the Langstons also worry about the potential adverse effects of various trends in health insurance programs on the family income, and that concern helps keep Doug's nose to the grindstone.

That is also why the Langstons have made it a point to invest in a diversified portfolio of marketable securities. Lately, however, two new investment opportunities have come their way, and suddenly, although they didn't know until we told them, they had put themselves on a clear runway toward perpetual wealth.

The first opportunity came from a colleague of Doug's, a fellow anesthesiologist who had devised a new piece of technology for medical practitioners. This innovative device helped anesthesiologists become more efficient in the operating room, and Doug agreed to invest in getting the device patented, piloted, and, when the pilot proved effective, manufactured. He went into partnership with the colleague—who now devotes himself full time to the company that makes the device while also experimenting with new technologies for anesthesiologists. Although the company has not yet turned a profit, Doug is so confident that it will that he finds himself searching for other new ideas that could advance the field he loves so much.

The other opportunity came when the Langstons' oldest son, a Navy officer who spends most of his time at sea, decided he wanted to buy some land in the Northeast—as a place to come home to some day. When he asked his parents for help in financing the purchase, it spurred the Langstons to do the same. They had always thought it would be a great idea to get a weekend place in the country, and they purchased a relatively large piece of land—large enough to divide into several large sites. They built their dream house on one, held another as mortgage holders to their son, and put the rest on the market, selling it at a nifty profit. They used the profit to buy more land plus a fixer-upper property, which they duly fixed up and have since rented out.

These two moves have set the Langstons firmly on the path to perpetual wealth. Since Doug's expertise in his anesthesiology practice, the source of most of his income, is not something he can pass on to his heirs, he can either sell his interest in his professional practice or the value of it will die with him. And while the income from his profession and diversified investment portfolio is certainly sufficient to keep the Langstons comfortable throughout Doug's working life and into retirement, it is not sufficient to ensure wealth for future generations to come. Thus, by reaching beyond the traditional investment in marketable securities—the typical professional's portfolio—into income-producing real estate and an innovative enterprise with which Doug can easily engage himself, the Langstons have ratcheted themselves up to a new level of wealth.

Doug still works hard—and loves his work—and the Langstons now have properties to manage and an innovative enterprise to worry about. But the financial risks they've assumed are manageable and acceptable, and the rewards, which are substantial, will keep on paying dividends long into the future.

CHAPTER 4

RISK AND THE ROAD TO WEALTH

As discussed in the previous chapter, creating your personal model to get rich, stay rich, and pass it on is no shell game, and it isn't achieved by sleight-of-hand. You cannot just move the shells around, switching assets from one pile to another—from annuities to real estate, or from securities to a privately held business—to match a "magic" percentage number on the benchmark model.

Creating the right model of perpetual wealth is not solely a quantitative exercise. We call it your *personal* model precisely because your personal circumstances, personal style, and personal preferences help shape it. That's why this chapter asks you to assess some highly individual matters. Specifically, you'll be tasked to measure your tolerance for risk and to evaluate your willingness to alter your investment activities.

Why is it important to know how much risk—and the kind of risk—you can tolerate and how ready you are to make changes in your investing style? Why not just barrel full steam ahead to match the benchmark percentages? Or turn it all over to your broker or financial advisor with instructions to "keep me informed"?

The first answer is, again, that this isn't a shell game. It isn't gambling. You are about to start structuring a plan to achieve perpetual wealth. That means investing for the very long term—past your years of working, even past your lifetime. It isn't something to be entered into lightly or without fore-thought and deliberation.

The second answer is that simply barreling ahead or turn-ing the whole process over to a third-party advisor simply won't work. Don't get us wrong: full steam ahead is a great way to move forward, and third-party advisors can be invaluable in helping you achieve perpetual wealth (as you will learn in Chapter 8), but neither is advisable unless—and until—you've laid the groundwork, and that means gaining the critical self-knowledge about your risk tolerance and your readiness to ef-fect change in various aspects of your life.

YOUR RISK TOLERANCE

How much risk can you handle? How much uncertainty are you equipped and ready to deal with? What downturn in the value of your assets is going to make you so uncomfortable as to make you lose sleep?

That's what the following quiz will help you to discover, and the discovery—the self-discovery—is critical. Knowing where you fit on the risk spectrum will help you decide how you invest as well as what you invest in. It will influence what you purchase, where you purchase it, and how you will allocate your assets.

Let's be clear: When we talk about risk, we are not talking about taking a flyer on some hot stock tip you got from a coworker who got it from his brother-in-law's cousin's dentist. That is not investing; it's gambling. Nor are we talking about the proverbial shell game in which assets are shuffled from one pocket to another.

When we talk about risk, we mean the classical definition of economics: "measurable uncertainty." We mean an acceptance on your part that investing can produce a range of possible outcomes, some negative and some positive. Risk tolerance, therefore, measures the level and kind of negative outcomes you'll accept in return for the level and kind of positive outcomes you seek.

Let's make something else perfectly clear at the outset: Some willingness to take risk is essential if you are going to gain the kind of wealth we've outlined throughout the book. That is because investing in both of the key activities that create such wealth—innovative enterprises and income-producing real estate—carries inherent risk. Our research has made it abundantly clear that it is difficult for the very risk-adverse to achieve perpetual wealth. It requires either very careful planning and great frugality, or a shift in attitude.

A shift in attitude may be required because risk tolerance is personality-specific and therefore a highly individual attribute. Precisely because it is a matter of individual personality, risk tolerance can vary according to age, income requirements, financial objectives, and personal circumstances. The twenty-five-year-old single investor is almost surely far more of a risk taker than the sixty-five-year-old widow on a pension.

But risk tolerance changes over time. In due course, that risk-taking twenty-five-year-old will very likely evolve into the risk-averse sixty-five-year-old, so his risk tolerance today may bear little resemblance to his risk tolerance 20 years from now. That is why your model for getting rich, staying rich, and passing it on will also change and evolve over time.

Still, our research has uncovered some general characteristics of risk tolerance, and while age and personality differences nuance these findings, they don't fundamentally change them. We have found, for example, that if you're a professional—a lawyer or doctor or corporate executive—you are more risk-averse than are business owners, real estate owners, and investors. If you fall into the former category, it is important to know that, to understand it, and to take it into account in building your perpetual wealth model.

Of course, a key factor in assessing risk—and therefore your risk tolerance—is the construct of time. Building a perpetual wealth model shifts the normal time horizon for risk. When you're aiming for perpetual wealth, losses may be recouped and returns realized well into the future. And while you may not be here to enjoy the full extent of the potential rewards, you also won't have to worry about the potential volatility. This is a reality that can affect an individual's tolerance for the risk involved in, for example, purchasing undeveloped real estate, or investing in small, capital-intensive businesses. It can also play a vital role when it comes to subsidizing emerging technologies, since the outcome of such speculative investments is such an unknown.

In fact, our research makes it clear that working the model for getting rich, staying rich, and passing it on is a lifetime's occupation—or in many cases, preoccupation. It's unlikely that you can build the model in a year, or even in five; certainly you will not see it yield a sustainable fortune in that amount of time. So you had better be comfortable with the risks you are taking, and you must also be prepared to reassess both the risks and your comfort level on a regular basis.

Our quiz will help you assess your risk tolerance level. The table that follows the quiz (see page 65) shows you where you fit on the risk spectrum compared to other types of investors. The table is based on our annual survey of thousands of investors which analyzes their stated attitudes and the realities of their investment activities.

For each question in the quiz, answer on a scale of 1 to 5, where 5 means you strongly agree with the statement and 1 means you strongly disagree. Of course, this is only useful if you are completely honest. Answer on the basis of what you really feel, not on the outcome you would like to achieve.

I AGREE/DISAGREE WITH THE FOLLOWING ATTITUDE	1 = DISAGREE WHOLEHEARTEDLY: 5 = AGREE WHOLEHEARTEDLY
1. I set aside a portion of my assets for more speculative or higher-risk investments.	
2. I expect my personal financial situation to be better a year from now.	
3. I would prefer to take chances with the equity markets rather than settle for a guaranteed rate of investment return.	
4. When the stock market is down, I look for buying opportunities.	
5. When the real estate market is down, I look for buying opportunities.	
TOTAL	

Then add up your total points. They will range from 5 to 30. Here's what your score tells you about your risk tolerance:

If you scored 15 or below, you are a conservative investor. Chances are you will find it too taxing—"too risky"—to invest in any meaningful way in income-producing real estate and/or to become a business owner. The bottom line? Unless you are a very careful planner and watch every penny, you will likely have much trouble achieving your model of perpetual wealth.

If you scored from 16 to 18, you are what we would call a moderate risk taker. That puts you in a category that our research indicates is chock full of professionals—lawyers, accountants, doctors—as well as many senior corporate executives. While these moderate risk takers may one day opt for aggressive investments, they do not do so without first expending substantial time and effort in analysis and deliberation. They need to push themselves a bit before they will take on more risk, but this group can tolerate some risk, and this makes them relatively strong candidates for starting down the path of the perpetually wealthy.

If you scored from 19 to 22, you are a more assertive investor. You are like the business owners and real estate investors that our research shows to be at the high end of moderate risk taking. Real estate investors in particular are typically on the lookout for investing opportunities, and when they do invest, they do so for the long term. Certainly, these high-end moderate risk takers conduct analyses of their investments and consider them carefully, but they have greater risk tolerance than the average doctor or corporate executive discussed in the previous category.

If you scored from 23 to 25, you have the perfect perpetual wealth personality. You are optimistic and willing to take on a relatively large degree of risk. You still carefully investigate real estate and entrepreneurial opportunities but are more willing to take the plunge than the investors in the previous three categories.

If you scored more than 25, you may qualify as an over-the-top investor. While a certain amount of aggressiveness is a necessary ingredient in the perpetual wealth model, being too willing to risk could be interpreted as reckless. Even if you manage to amass enough wealth to pass it on, your recklessness may very well prevent you from holding on to it. If you fit into this category, we suggest that you acknowledge that now and carefully document and track all of your investments to make sure that you are not leaking money on a regular basis.

Where Do You Stand on the Risk Tolerance Spectrum—and with Whom?

CONSERVATIVE	MODERATE RISK TAKER				EXTREME RISK TAKER
5	10	15	20	25	30

Senior Executives

Professionals

Real Estate Investors

Business Owners

Perpetual Wealth Personality

Over-the Top Investors

MAKING THE TOUGH CHANGES

How good are you at making meaningful changes in your life? If you find it tough, you're in good company. Most psychologists agree that change is never easy. The classic example is that of cardiac patients instructed to modify their lifestyle or risk deterioration—or worse. Most find it notoriously difficult to undo old habits and initiate new ones; many—far too many— fail in the attempt. It is a costly and very final failure.

The changes you'll be making in your investment habits aren't quite as momentous as the changes demanded of heart patients, nor will the outcome be a matter of life or death. Still, the chances are good that using the two secrets to getting rich, staying rich, and passing it on will mean a substantial change—even a radical change—in your overall investment portfolio and therefore in your financial life. The changes in your investment life will almost assuredly trigger other changes in the rest of your life as well. After all, to gain a fortune that lasts virtually forever, you'll have to focus time, energy, and money on activities you likely have not participated in before.

You will need to get involved in owning, managing, or actively investing in real estate; if your current real estate involvement is limited only to your principal residence, then owning income-producing real estate will mean a substantial change. In fact, the benchmark model calls for you to allocate some 23 percent to 29 percent of your wealth to real estate. That's going to require a parallel investment of time and attention as well.

Moreover, our research shows that 8 percent to 13 percent of your real estate investing needs to be in properties that now, or in the future, have the potential to generate income for you and your heirs. In this regard, a healthy combination of residential, commercial, and vacant land held for future building is an ideal investment vehicle.

If selecting and purchasing such a collection of properties is not difficult enough, they also have to be managed. That might mean getting up in the middle of the night to answer an irate phone call from a hysterical tenant with a plumbing problem, or fielding a call from another tenant with a heating outage. If that is not for you, you may opt to hire a property management agency, particularly if the properties are in far-flung locations where you cannot keep as close an eye on them as you'd like. This adds another element of risk to the mix.

Following the other secret to perpetual wealth will also significantly impact your current lifestyle. Our benchmark model of perpetual wealth dictates that between 25 percent to 35 percent of investment assets be in the form of innovative companies. Making such an investment will require you to focus on enterprises that develop new products and services or invent breakthrough technologies. Chances are you've never struck out in such a direction before. Doing so now will therefore require change.

That's why it's important to assess your readiness for change—your willingness to alter your investment pattern and your financial activities going forward. We've created an exercise that will help you make that assessment.

Based on our research, we've created scenarios for five families and ranked them in terms of their real estate activities and their involvement in continually innovative enterprises. We've scored each family on a scale of 1 to 10, depending upon how likely it is that the family's current situation will put it on track to perpetual wealth.

We also score how long the current wealth scenario will

last—that is, how many generations will enjoy the family's wealth given the current scenario. And we suggest the investment activities each family might implement over time to improve its chances for perpetual wealth. Read the entire chart through, and then figure out which family scenario most closely resembles your own.

Your Readiness for Getting Rich, Staying Rich, and Passing It On: Which Family Scenario Best Resembles Yours?

1. THE JONES FAMILY

Scenario: The family's current investment activities

- Primary residence is only real estate investment.
- Investments are primarily in marketable assets.
- Do not own or invest continually in innovative private businesses.

How likely (scale of 1–10) is it that this scenario will bring the family to perpetual wealth?

1–2

How many generations will this family's wealth survive under the current scenario of investment activities?

1

What kinds of investment activities should the family implement to raise its scenario scorecard closer to a '"Perfect 10"?

- Over a period of years, slowly realign investment activities by shifting assets away from marketable securities to either a second home or into income-producing real estate. Consider investing with friends or family members for first real estate venture.
- Assess current career interest and aspirations to determine likelihood of career change into investing in and managing an innovative business. If career change is realistic, network with advisors, friends, and family to seek out innovative ventures or ideas, then consider acquiring the company or starting a new venture related to the idea. Do homework and start small.
- If a career change is not realistic, network with advisors, friends, and family to identify investment opportunities. The aim: Gain investment exposure and sense of "ownership" in private innovative businesses.

2. THE SMITH FAMILY

Scenario: The family's current investment activities

- Primary residence is only real estate investment.
- Partial owner of private innovative business.

How likely (scale of 1–10) is it that this scenario will bring the family to perpetual wealth?

3–4

How many generations will this family's wealth survive under the current scenario of investment activities?

1

What kinds of investment activities should the family implement to raise its scenario scorecard closer to a '"Perfect 10"?

- Keep up with the Joneses: Slowly realign investment activities over time by shifting assets away from marketable securities to either a second home or into income-producing real estate. Consider investing with friends or family members for first real estate venture.
- If not currently owner of property in which business is based, evaluate the viability of purchasing the location, or consider purchasing another property and/or facility where business can be relocated. Occupy portion of facility and rent out remaining facility to develop income stream from real estate.
- Leverage ownership in privately held innovative business into other ventures in which there is expertise so as to grow the business faster, or develop new ventures in which a greater interest is owned.

3. THE JOHNSON FAMILY

Scenario: The family's current investment activities

- Primary residence and second home represent 15% of overall investment activity.
- Do not own a portion of a private business.

How likely (scale of 1–10) is it that this scenario will bring the family to perpetual wealth?

5–6

How many generations will this family's wealth survive under the current scenario of investment activities?

2

What kinds of investment activities should the family implement to raise its scenario scorecard closer to a '"Perfect 10"?

- Increase investment activity in real estate over time by investing in income-producing property to a level closer to the benchmark model. As the Jones family is doing, assess current career interest and aspirations to determine likelihood of career change into investing and managing an innovative business. If career change is realistic, network with advisors, friends, and family to seek out innovative ventures to consider acquiring, or explore other areas in which to start a new venture. Do homework and start small.
- If career change is not realistic, network with advisors, friends, and family to identify investment opportunities. The aim: Gain some investment exposure and sense of "ownership" in private innovative businesses.

4. THE GREENE FAMILY

Scenario: The family's current investment activities

- Real estate holdings represent 20% of overall assets and include income-producing assets.
- Partial owner of a private innovative business.

How likely (scale of 1–10) is it that this scenario will bring the family to perpetual wealth?

7–8

How many generations will this family's wealth survive under the current scenario of investment activities?

2–3

What kinds of investment activities should the family implement to raise its scenario scorecard closer to a '"Perfect 10"?

- Through acquisitions, gradually expand real estate investment to at least 23% of total investment activities.
- As the Smiths are doing, leverage ownership in private business into other ventures in which there is expertise so as to grow the business, or develop new ventures in which a greater interest is owned.

5. THE MARK FAMILY

Scenario: The family's current investment activities

- Real estate investment represents 25–28% of total assets and includes: primary residence, second and third homes, incoming-producing properties, and REITs.
- Majority owner of large private innovative firm.

How likely (scale of 1–10) is it that this scenario will bring the family to perpetual wealth?

9–10

How many generations will this family's wealth survive under the current scenario of investment activities?

3–5

What kinds of investment activities should the family implement to raise its scenario scorecard closer to a '"Perfect 10"?

- Actively manage real estate investments. Continually evaluate appropriateness of second and third homes. For example, if ski house is no longer used following retirement to Florida, think about selling it— unless still used regularly by children and grandchildren. Similarly, continually review location of investment properties. If property is in a once-vibrant neighborhood that is now in decline, think about replacing it with a building in a better area in order to maintain an income stream, but relocate to raise the inherent value of holdings.
- Ensure that innovative company remains innovative and continually reinvents itself to serve the marketplace of the future.

HOW THE RICH THINK ABOUT RISK

Want to know where you stand vis-à-vis those who have already achieved perpetual wealth? As you may suspect, risk tolerance seems to diminish with age. Moreover, attitudes toward risk vary between risk takers and those who are risk averse. Where do you fit in these contexts?

- Twelve percent of individuals over the age of sixty-five consider themselves as "conservative" and "seek stable returns." Only 3 percent of individuals under age fifty-five characterize themselves like that.

- Seventy-nine percent of individuals that consider themselves to be a "risk taker" want to build rather than preserve wealth. Ninety-two percent of "risk takers" set aside a portion of their assets for speculative investments and only 28 percent of "risk takers" seek a guaranteed return on some investments. Forty-nine percent of "non-risk takers" want a guaranteed return on investment.

Now that you've done the exercises in this and the previous chapters, you've laid the groundwork for creating your personal perpetual wealth model. You've been introduced to the benchmark model that will guide you as you begin to create your own model. You've dimensioned the financial difference between your current financial profile and the profile of the perpetually rich. And you've assessed where you fit on the risk-reward spectrum and how ready you are in terms of time and effort to put your family on the path to perpetual wealth.

It's time to start writing the script for your personal model of perpetual wealth.

A PORTRAIT OF PERPETUAL WEALTH:
THE HARD-WORKING ENTREPRENEUR

No one ever handed Tom Kramer a free pass. He took over the small family snow "digging" business when his father was killed suddenly in the car crash that also gravely injured his mother. Under the law, the company accounts were frozen, and the company cash could not be accessed. "I had $5,000 to keep the business going," Tom says. "I didn't know how long I would make it."

That's when he began sleeping in the pickup so he could be first out of the gate to clear snow in the morning; being first, after all, meant he could do a greater number of jobs in the course of a day. Tom kept it up until he had enough money to hire a coworker to handle the night shift. Then he concentrated on capturing long-term snowplowing contracts with some of the new corporate offices and retail malls being built in his region of the Midwest.

But Tom knew that moving snow wasn't going to be enough—even in a part of the country where there seemed to be only two seasons: July and winter. During the fuel crisis of the 1970s, Tom took advantage of investment credits to upgrade his equipment. He didn't do it alone. Instead, he established relationships with a lawyer and an accountant who could help him not just buy equipment but plan and meet some long-range financial goals.

His wife, Carol, had been "keeping the books," but she had to give up those duties to raise their three children full time. And Tom knew he didn't have the expertise to work his way through the legal and financial thicket of high-level financing, acquisitions, and the like. So he did his homework and hired on two top-notch advisors to tackle the financial end of things.

Right out of the box, Tom knew he had to make several important decisions in order to grow the company. He realized he needed more space for the equipment he had, not to mention for the equipment he hoped to buy down the line. He felt strongly that the property across the street would fit the bill, but Tom's mother and brother, still beneficiaries of the business, were opposed to the purchase; they wanted to move slowly and didn't like the idea of taking on new responsibilities. With the help of his lawyer and accountant, Tom made the tough decision to buy out his mother and brother and make the property purchase he deemed so important. Sure enough, the business kept growing.

Tom kept buying real estate. He bought a nearby property that he thought would be perfect for a fast-food franchise, but he changed his mind when he learned of the steep franchise fee structure, and instead rented the property to a local ice cream store. However, that business soon failed. Clearly, there would be no more rent from this investment. Since the property had been substantively modified to accommodate the ice cream store, Tom approached another local ice cream provider, one that was already doing well in the area. They struck a deal: Tom took a percentage of ownership in the business in exchange for the use of the property. The business succeeded, and both sides profited.

Tom kept adjusting his business, and he kept

on buying real estate—including the swampland he dumped dirt on. The "digging" business evolved into a major excavation outfit that also offers snowplowing and related services. The company is also the sole firm in the region that grinds concrete—and Tom has found that being the only game in town can be highly profitable.

Recently, Tom's youngest son, one of two who joined the business, persuaded his father to use the Web to handle the business's increasingly complex administrative tasks. Now billing, proposals, logistics, and the like are wholly automated. Tom had to smile when he realized how far he had come from the days he slept in the pickup.

Tom Kramer now has a three-tiered wealth model: entrepreneurial investment in his own small business, investments in other promising businesses, and smart investments in various kinds of real estate. Tom was unafraid to reach out for expert help and advice to smooth the path and he also relied on his own intuition.

Tom's intuition is still sound. Recently, the swamp where he dumped dirt sold to a large retailer for a fortune. And Tom recently "negotiated" a deal to buy a $250,000 tractor for $220,000. How? Knowing that the dealership closed at noon on a Saturday, Tom showed up at 11:30 and offered $220,000 in cash, take it or leave it.

The dealer took it. Chalk up an extra $30,000 for the Kramer generations yet to come.

CHAPTER 5

THE FIRST SECRET OF PERPETUAL WEALTH

Unless you are a nomad, a transient, or a full-time seafarer, chances are good that you own or rent a home. So does just about everybody in most developed countries. Certainly it can be said that the overwhelming majority of today's 300 million Americans own or rent a place in which to live.

That is a simplistic statement, but in fact it reflects an essential economic fact: The very substantive value of real estate is that everybody needs it. Shelter is one of humankind's basic needs, after all—along with food and clothing. And it isn't only individuals and families that require shelter. So do businesses, shops, schools, ball teams, governments, nongovernmental organizations, moviegoers, the bridge club, the country club, the United Nations, the Girl or Boy Scouts, and the list goes on.

What's more, shelter is required in fine weather as well as foul, in warm climates as well as cold, through boom times and depression, inflation and recession. No matter what, buildings and the land on which they're built are a profound part of the human condition in the twenty-first century—certainly in the industrialized world. So while the price of real estate may fluctuate due to changing market and economic conditions and the law of supply and demand, its inherent value persists.

There are various ways to measure that value. If you rent your home, the value you are getting for your money is a place to live—no small thing. If you own your home, you probably measure its value in equity, or the residual value of the property, which is its current market value minus whatever mortgage liability you still carry on it.

Where perpetual wealth is concerned, however, the real estate value that counts is a property's ability to produce income. Having a place to live is essential, of course, and building up a nest egg with the equity in your home is a fine thing. But what distinguishes the model for getting rich, staying rich, and passing it on is its emphasis on investing in current and future income-producing real estate—to the tune, in fact, of some 8 percent to 13 percent of the total investment portfolio. It is this particular investment—both the scope of it and its income-producing potential—that sets the perpetually wealthy apart from all other holders of wealth, even the megarich.

REAL ESTATE INVESTMENTS OF THE VERY RICH

The research results supporting this conclusion are consistent and dramatic. We continually measure the investment habits of the wealthiest Americans—the mega-millionaire households. Year after year, this group—with obvious potential for creating perpetual wealth—has maintained substantial investment in real estate. It's worthwhile reviewing that investment and detailing its fine points.

First, let's recall from Chapter 2 that more than three-quarters of the mega-millionaire households in the United States were invested in income-producing real estate.

Moreover, as we've stated repeatedly, they were *heavily* invested. One more time: The average real estate investment among mega-millionaire households came to $2.9 million per investor, and the wealthier the household, the greater percentage its real estate investments.

There is a slightly different pattern of real estate investment between business owners and professionals—two key blocs among mega-millionaire households and two key blocs of the perpetually wealthy. As we have seen, the data reveal that business owners raise the curve on real estate investment while professionals lower it a bit (a matter of personality, risk tolerance, and financial habits), yet the average between the two is still a substantial amount of investment—confirmation that the focus on real estate is a distinctive marker for achieving perpetual wealth.

Even more important than the pervasiveness of real estate investment is the type of real estate investment choices made by these very wealthy investors—and the way in which they allocate their investment among the different options. Second homes, third homes, undeveloped land, rental properties, Real Estate Investment Trusts (REITs), even time-shares and vacation clubs are all in the running for the real estate investment dollars of mega-millionaire households. And while second homes constitute the most common option chosen, rental properties, offering a regular income on a sustained basis, are a close second.

The research also demonstrates that the richer you are, the more you invest in rental properties. The top ranks of mega-millionaire real estate investors averaged some $5.8 million per investor in rental properties, at least twice as much as in undeveloped land, REITs, or any other kinds of real estate investment.

The research tells us something else. Among the wealthiest Americans, investment in real estate is seen as a long-term proposition. We know this not only from attitude surveys but from the data we've collected: You're not going to invest this much of your total assets in these dollar amounts this consistently on a dare, a hot tip, or a highly risky venture. While there is no such thing as a sure thing, real estate has proven to be as solid an investment as there is *over the long term*. The very, very rich know that—and the perpetually wealthy rely on it.

So if this is how—and how much—the wealthy invest in real estate, how should you approach it? In what kinds of properties should you invest as you start creating your personal model to get rich, stay rich, and pass it on? How much money should you invest? And how do you begin?

START WHERE YOU LIVE—LITERALLY

Step One is to define your starting line, and the best place to find it is at home. Literally.

For one thing, in the most practical sense, your home is very likely your launch pad to investing in income-producing real estate. Why? Because you can leverage the equity you have in your home to purchase income-producing properties. If you own the single-family home in which you live, sit down right now and determine exactly how much equity you have in this essential piece of real estate.

In figuring out your equity, make sure the market value you assign to the house—before subtracting the mortgage you still owe on it—is real. It should be based on an appraisal or a professionally executed comparative market analysis—*not* on what the house next door sold for last year, or what you wish the market value of the house was, or what friends assure you it ought to be. The real market value is a real number, and unless it is accurately stated, you won't get a true picture of the equity in the property.

That equity is your point of departure; the aim will be to leverage your existing equity to buy your "next" property—and property after property—thus ensuring both income production and the further enhancement of your equity position.

But suppose you rent the home you live in—a house or an apartment or a condo—and have no equity at all. How can you leverage "up" to buy that first piece of income-producing real estate?

One very basic solution is to buy a two-family house, live in one side of it and rent out the other. In that way, your tenant is helping you build equity by paying you a monthly amount that offsets expenses while you build the needed equity to begin your program of real estate investment. Of course, you could also simply buy a rental property while continuing to pay your own rent on your current residence. In this case, you are building equity in the property you buy while leaving yourself free to choose how and where you want to live.

This brings us to the second reason that starting a real estate investment program where you live makes perfect sense:

Where you live is what you know. An urbanite will almost surely be a less-than-savvy investor in undeveloped farmland; conversely, a farmer is unlikely to have a clue about investing in properties in the downtown area of a major city. And while there are certainly experts and advisors aplenty to help with such choices, it makes sense, especially when beginning to formulate your personal model for getting rich, staying rich, and passing it on, to go with what you know—good advice whenever money is the issue.

THE SECOND HOME

By far the most common "next" real estate purchase people make is a second home. City folks seek seclusion in the countryside. Flatlanders head for the mountains. Cold-weather dwellers look for beachfront cottages.

A second home is a haven, a refuge, a recreational paradise, a remote office, a chance at another way of life—none of the things we associate with income production. So how can a second home fit in your perpetual wealth model?

First of all, a second home, like the first, is an equity builder. And equity, as we have said, is the launching pad for financing the purchase of other properties that will produce income. But a second home may also be a part-time rental property, and this is an option increasingly being exercised— helped immeasurably by the Internet.

Take the case of a musician we'll call Larry. When he first started out in his twenties, his career was almost entirely "on the road," and he lived in a succession of short-term sublets and hotel rooms. Eager to have a place he could one day "come home to," but not exactly flush with money, Larry managed to save just enough for a down payment on a modest A-frame log cabin on a hilltop in an economically depressed area about three hours outside New York City.

When he met Sabine, one of the things he loved most about her was how much she loved his funky hideaway in the middle of nowhere, and when they married, the hideaway became their real home—as well as storage room for the things that just wouldn't fit into their tiny New York studio.

But then Larry's career started to take off. Cabaret was big again; he got a virtually permanent weekend gig at one of New York's hottest clubs just before a recording company signed him to a contract. Sabine gave up her own career teaching dance when their son and daughter were born, and the family moved out of the tiny studio and into a suburban house across the river in New Jersey. The upstate A-frame, appreciating in value every year, stayed empty most of the time.

So Larry and Sabine decided to rent it out. Since musicians work when others play—always on holidays, especially Christmas and New Year—and since the A-frame was five minutes from a ski center, it was easy to rent it out for the ski season. Then they began renting it for long weekends when Larry was working—Thanksgiving, Memorial Day, and Columbus Day, when the fall foliage was at its peak. Then they discovered a range of vacation rental sites on the Internet—www.vacation rentals.com, www.vrbo.com, www.vacationhomerentals.com, www.cyberrentals.com, and of course, www.craigslist.com— and simply began listing dates when the house would be available. They always found tenants—always, for whatever time of year and whatever period of time they chose to make the house available for rent.

Larry says they wouldn't think of selling the place, even though they now use it only a few weeks a year. But they still love being there when they can, expect to retire there someday, and besides, it pays for itself and provides them additional income as well. The rents they receive—for a weekend, a week, fishing season, ski season, etc.—cover their mortgage payments and all carrying charges plus all the costs of maintenance, like the new roof and external restaining they had done one summer. It has also helped them buy a cottage in France, Sabine's home country, which they also rent out, using it only during their annual visits to see her family.

A neighbor down the road does the same thing Larry and Sabine do—but in reverse. Sarah owns a New York condo apartment and a small cabin on the shoulder of a hill. The cabin is her getaway, although the city remains her primary residence. But it is both easy and lucrative to rent out a Manhattan apartment for all those occasions during which Sarah chooses to flee the city: holidays, summer vacations, and in the dead-of-winter when Sarah wants to be skiing and tourists want to attend Broadway shows. Although the income is seasonal, and although her annual take varies depending on when Sarah is willing to give up time in New York, it represents a very welcome addition to the compensation package she gets at work—a nice nest egg, and a good start toward a model of wealth that lasts.

SHARED INVESTMENT

Can you realize these benefits of second home ownership with a time-share? Not even close. Time-shares offer the possibility of affordable vacations and may be cost-effective if your family or time-share group is large. But you get no equity from your time-share, no appreciation—and of course, no income.

Still, the idea of sharing an investment certainly has merit. Unlike Larry, who was able to look only for a house in an economically depressed area, you may be able to join with friends to buy and share a "second" or vacation home of a size and/or in an area you simply would not be able to afford on your own.

We know three guys who got together shortly after college, pooled what resources they had, and managed to purchase a vacation home in Hawaii. They came up with a pretty simple arrangement for sharing the use of the place: Since there were three of them, each would be entitled to four months a year to use the place as he saw fit. The first year, the first in line would get January, April, July, and October, while the second would start his rotation in February and the third in March; the second year, the first in line would start his three-month rotation in February; the third year, his three months would begin in March, and so on.

Of course, some of the men decided to rent out all or part of their shares some of the time; that was their right, and the income was all theirs. Meanwhile, all house maintenance and repair costs were equally shared.

The arrangement, though simple, has proven sound; it has worked for more than 30 years. During that time, of course, the value of the investment has appreciated considerably, building equity for each of the three owners, while those who rented out all or part of their four-month stints—as all did at one time or other—realized welcome income from their share in the property as well.

As this example illustrates, shared investments can provide all the benefits of owning an income-producing property, albeit on a narrower basis than full ownership, while also splitting the burden of ownership—that is, responsibility for maintenance and repair, insurance and taxes. The key to it is the arrangement among the sharing owners. Responsibilities, liabilities, and benefits should be absolutely clear. We can't recommend too strongly that you seek the services of a good lawyer to draw up a contract that all parties will be happy with, can live with, and that delineates all their obligations with airtight clarity and perfect equality.

COMMERCIAL REAL ESTATE

In its most basic form, investing in commercial real estate is no different than buying a house and renting it out. By "basic," we mean buying a small storefront that you lease to a business owner, or perhaps buying space in the building in which you work—or a similar office space—and renting it out to a commercial tenant much like yourself.

It's when you go beyond this simple, single-unit kind of property that commercial real estate can become complicated. Of course, that's also when it becomes particularly rewarding as well.

What complicates commercial real estate ownership is

not just numbers but also the kinds of transactions required for owning and managing these properties, which tend to be quite different in character from the kinds of transactions with which homeowners are familiar. Owning a building or warehouse in which numerous businesses and/or retail stores can rent space, or a hotel or multiresidential building—an apartment complex, for example—multiplies the transactions of ownership and management considerably. But it also means multiple covenants as well as multiple leases, multiple and diverse arrangements concerning payment of utilities, taxes, insurance, common area maintenance, and the like.

It means managing maintenance and repair issues particular to industrial or office buildings or malls or hotels that are far different from a leaky roof or a blown fuse in a single-family house. It means knowing what you are doing and/or being sure to deal with reputable experts in the field—including lawyers, brokers, and accountants who specialize in commercial real estate.

For this reason—not to mention cost—commercial real estate is another area in which sharing an investment with friends, family, or like-minded investors is a good idea. A purchase price that you could not manage on your own, plus management responsibilities that would be overly burdensome for you alone, may all become possible if the investment is shared. Again, if you enter into a shared investment in commercial real estate, make sure your own attorney goes to bat for you in finalizing the details of the share arrangement.

UNDEVELOPED LAND

Buying undeveloped land is a gamble that can pay off substantially—but only if you guess right, and your chances of guessing right are vastly improved if you know the area and the type of land you are buying, and practice patience, which is absolutely essential. In fact, when buying undeveloped land—perhaps more than in any other investment—the key to success is to buy it and hold it. The problem is that while you're holding it, undeveloped land costs you money. Real estate taxes and liability insurance will be the primary expenses, and they can be substantial.

There are some ways to offset the punch of those expenses. In some states, buying and holding agricultural land and/or forested land may be, to some extent, subsidized. Stewardship projects, forestry and farmland trusts, conservation easements, and other programs are in place across the nation to compensate owners for serving as stewards of land that may have intrinsic value in providing water or soil protection, scenic view shed, or environmental and/or recreational potential.

Again, this brings home the point that it is essential to know what you are buying—in terms of both geography and the use to which the land can be put. Don't count on being able to reduce the tax bite on undeveloped land anywhere under all circumstances. Find out if there is a program you can qualify for before you make your purchase.

BUILDING WEALTH—LITERALLY

Neither Alan Hall nor his wife, Lillian, ever went to college. After high school, Alan followed his father into the building trades as a carpenter and contractor. Lillian, a farmer's daughter, was a stay-at-home wife and mother, although by now she has become as erudite and expert an investment analyst as there is in the industry.

Alan and Lillian live in a ranch-style home in a rural area of the Midwest. Alan built the house himself some 30 years ago, and just about every year he devises some new project that lets him add yet another feature to the home. His innovations have included a goldfish pond with a bridge over it leading to the front door, a bricked fire pit surrounded by a garden for parties, a screened-in porch, surrounded by trees, that overlooks a vast ravine.

In his cavernous workshop, Alan enjoys carpentry and woodcrafting or just puttering away on one project or another. The workshop is leftover from the business from which Alan recently retired—a highly successful contractor partnership.

The partnership dates to the mid-1970s when Alan became interested in a piece of land immediately across the road from the home he had just built. He was introduced to a young mason who was also interested in the land. They formed a partnership and purchased the land through a bank loan, then developed it into a subdivision. The bank loan was paid off within a year; neither Alan nor his partner ever believed in debt.

The subdivision was cut into more than 40 lots, all

of which sold. Alan and his new partner then formed a company that built many of the homes in the subdivision and they became well known throughout the region for the diversity of their homes and for the quality of their construction. The partnership lasted until the two retired.

The company was small, but the revenues were significant, and costs were low. The partners invested their profits in local real estate—commercial buildings, duplexes, and residences. Alan also invested on his own. At one point, the local bank even approached him for investment funding. Alan said yes, and when the bank was acquired by a large national bank, he was handsomely rewarded.

All in all, buying and developing land has brought the Halls a level of wealth they never dreamed possible in their early life together, and it just keeps paying off.

They've invested in numerous other markets and projects as well. Lillian enjoys spending her time reviewing and researching the couple's investments, although they also depend on a full-service broker for much of their financial advice, especially where stocks and bonds are concerned. They like the broker, knew his father, know his children, and trust him implicitly. When the broker changed firms, they followed him to his new company—more than once. Lillian doesn't always accept his recommendations, but she believes they are based on sound fundamentals.

Not surprisingly for this conscientious couple, the Halls have a fully developed estate plan. Trusts have been established for their son as well as for their grandchildren. "I feel good because I know my grandchildren's education is taken care of," says Lillian. Now that they're retired, the Halls are also beginning to focus on liquidating some of their real estate holdings on the theory that liquid securities will be easier for their heirs to manage.

Both Halls are healthy and fit individuals. Lillian walks every day and likes to focus her energy on healthy eating; she has taken courses and has educated herself in the subject of nutrition. Always an avid reader, she has also educated herself in spectacular fashion on the subject of finance. As a result, it is she who analyzes and decides about their real estate investments, who manages their savings, and who continually monitors the great wealth the Halls have built—almost literally— building by building.

REITS

Up to this point we have discussed the kind of tangible real estate one can literally live on or find on a map. But what if you are not familiar with the area in which real estate is available— whether it is undeveloped land or highly developed residential or commercial real estate? Or what if you know the area but don't know what's available to invest in—or whether it's worth investing in?

And what if, in addition, you really don't want to do the necessary research or homework but you still want to strike out on this essential track toward perpetual wealth? Real Estate

Investment Trusts—REITs, which rhymes with "streets"—may be the solution.

A Real Estate Investment Trust, as its name implies, is a fund, or pool, of real estate investments—much the same as a mutual fund is a fund or pool of stocks. In fact, REITs are sometimes referred to as real estate stocks. Unsecured and illiquid, a REIT is a long-term investment—typically 20 years at the least.

There are three basic types of REIT. An equity REIT owns and manages income-producing real estate of all property types; by investing in it, you are paying equity to buy properties chosen by professionals while the income returns to the trust. Mostly, equity REITs own and operate commercial properties—office buildings, industrial buildings, mixed-use buildings, shopping centers and malls, hotels and resorts, etc.—but residential buildings also make up a portion of the typical equity REIT portfolio.

Mortgage REITs finance these real estate investments, either by lending money directly to investors or by acquiring mortgages or mortgage-backed securities.

Hybrid REITs, as the name makes clear, do both: they own properties and they finance property ownership.

Some REITs—of all three types—provide an annual income; others do not pay off until the end of the time period of your shares. Most require some sort of minimum investment, but the minimum varies from fund to fund.

For general investment purposes, REIT returns are considered an important tool of diversification since they show little correlation to the stock market; that is, whether the stock market goes up or down has no effect on the dividend yields from REITs. (Although their dividend yields are not affected by the market, their overall price may have some correlation to the market as a whole.)

For purposes of creating your personal model of perpetual wealth, REITs are a good way to get into the real estate investment market at an affordable "entry fee" and without having to do the hard work of researching and analyzing markets. However, our research shows that almost 100 percent of the perpetually wealthy are involved with "hard" real estate of one kind or another. Still, REITs may be a good way for you to get into the water before diving into the deep end.

However you become an investor in real estate, the goal is to build that investment to somewhere between 23 percent to 29 percent of your total investment portfolio. When you have achieved that, you will have mastered one of the secrets to getting rich, staying rich, and passing it on. Mastering the other secret, investing in continually innovative enterprises, may prove a bit more challenging and a bit more difficult to achieve. The truth, however, is that once you know how, it isn't difficult at all.

A PORTRAIT OF PERPETUAL WEALTH: CIRCUMSPECT BY NATURE

"Be a doctor when you grow up," mothers like to tell their children. "Or a lawyer. That way you can take care of all of us."

Ronda Lewis heard the message but didn't buy into it—at least, not at first. Instead, this highly educated California attorney, originally from Louisiana, pursued a Ph.D. in English before attending law school, and she enrolled in the latter as much for her intense interest in law as for the long-term benefits of the professional lifestyle. That's Ronda's character: studious, methodical, in love with content and problem solving. It's no wonder, in fact, that in addition to her highly successful legal practice, Ronda today teaches research and writing at a local law school.

Ronda met Tom Lewis at the big law firm they both worked for right out of law school. Experts in eminent domain—that is, the lawful appropriation of private property by the government for what is claimed to be a public purpose—the two eventually spun off their own specialist practice, founded their own law firm, and made it a rousing success, achieving a level of wealth that astounded them both. Two children followed, and Ronda made the choice to work only part time at the firm, teach at the law school, and keep a flexible schedule for the children.

Typical of professionals, the two decided it was time to develop a long-range financial plan. Also typical of professionals, they discovered that they both had an aversion to risk, and that their paramount concerns were for their future security and the education of their children. After consulting with the financial planning department of their accountant's firm, they invested a large sum of money in a defined benefit plan set up exclusively for their children's college education.

Ronda feels good about the investment, but she

continues to have serious concerns about their future financial security. Founding a law firm was a wrenching adventure for her, going against her naturally conservative nature. She is aware that, like many professionals, she lacks the kind of sales and marketing skills that seem to come naturally to entrepreneurs and business owners. She also suspects that, despite the firm's success, the highly specialized nature of the Lewises' law practice is limiting, and she worries that the huge case on which the firm has expended so much time and so many resources has also cost it the opportunity to recruit more new business.

In addition, she anticipates that Tom may be facing a midlife career change. "There's no urgency," she says, "but he's looking for a sense of purpose," and legal work seems less and less able to supply that for him.

Ronda worries the most, however, about getting into debt, aware that all of her other concerns—the firm's future, Tom's midlife crisis, business building—"cost money."

The idea of investing in real estate came to the Lewises almost by accident. Tom's parents had bought units in an apartment building, and then had parlayed the investment into ownership and part-ownership of a string of buildings. When Tom's father became ill with Alzheimer's, more and more of the work of managing both the investments and the buildings fell to Ronda. After putting in place the requisite trusts and estate-planning tools, she found herself spending a lot of time wrestling with tenant complaints.

Although managing the properties was time-consuming, it instilled in Ronda a familiarity and level of comfort with the whole idea of real estate and mitigated some of her natural risk aversion. So when presented with the chance to invest through limited real estate partnerships in both California and Las Vegas, Ronda seized the opportunity with some measure of enthusiasm.

The perpetually worried Ronda Lewis may not seem like anybody's idea of a progenitor of perpetual wealth. Guarded, tentative, reluctant to take on risk, and disinclined to take chances with innovation, she nevertheless represents all the potential for realizing a sustainable fortune. Her one innovative enterprise, the law firm she founded with Tom, has achieved substantive wealth and has enabled Ronda to craft a lifestyle she finds both personally and professionally satisfying. With Tom thinking of giving up the law, it is possible the firm may be sold, offering another significant financial opportunity and the possibility of involvement in a new innovative enterprise. They've done it once; that could conceivably help convince them they could do it again.

Now the expansion of their real estate investments is providing them "practice" in moving beyond their law practice—and perhaps beyond Ronda's caution and Tom's passivity. They know firsthand that the rents coming in from their parents' apartments can provide ongoing income, while their own current investments can be leveraged to supplement their existing defined benefit plan. That has spurred them to invest farther afield both geographically and in property types as they buy into strip malls and other properties in the growing Mountain West region. That's half the prescription to getting rich, staying rich, and passing it on—and it's a formidable beginning.

But they need to investigate the second secret as well, and for that, their best opportunity may be found in Tom's dissatisfaction with his legal career. Although he is uncertain how to change it, and although his "professional" nature makes him slow to venture into new initiatives, Tom's search for a new enterprise could propel the couple into investing in the kind of continually innovative enterprise that could plant them firmly on the path to perpetual wealth.

CHAPTER 6

THE SECOND SECRET
OF PERPETUAL WEALTH

When you're looking to invest in real estate, the signs are fairly obvious; they're brightly colored, they line local roads, and they communicate a clear message: For Sale.

The signs won't be nearly that visible when you're searching for continually innovative enterprises in which to get involved. The opportunities won't fall into your lap quite as readily as that perfect piece of real estate might. Uncovering this secret to getting rich, staying rich, and passing it on is probably going to take much more time and effort than investing in real estate, but it is of course equally essential.

How do you find—or create—a continually innovative enterprise? And once you've identified the enterprise, how and how much should you invest? Before we can answer those questions, we need to define our terms.

THE "CONTINUALLY INNOVATIVE ENTERPRISE" DEFINED

Even defining the continually innovative enterprise isn't easy, for an understanding of the phrase "continually innovative" is more subjective than scientific. What we mean here by a continually innovative enterprise is one that either offers a product or service that breaks new ground or changes a traditional product or service so much that it becomes virtually new.

Ideally, the enterprise continues to reinvent either the product or service itself, the means of delivering the product or service, or the means of managing the enterprise. The result is that the enterprise maintains its edge in its market or industry, or simply in its inherent purpose.

Our economy today is dominated by an industry—technology—in which constant innovation is *expected,* and is indeed required. Consider these examples:

- Apple, with its steady stream of high-concept, consumer-friendly designs (think iPod);

- Dell, whose innovations in cost-cutting and supply-chain management has brought a new level of affordable quality to the computer market;

- And of course, Google, with its ongoing creation of new tools and services that have revolutionized the Internet search so dramatically that its name, Google, has now become a verb.

The trick, of course, is to find the Apples and Dells and Googles before they become household words—and behemoths in their industry.

It isn't only the technology industry that sprouts continual innovation. Less dramatic but equally valid are the examples of some other large, well-known corporations that have continually innovated; that's usually how they got to be large and well known. Sears is a classic case.

Starting as a retailer of watches, the Sears enterprise went on to invent the mail-order catalog, thus creating a whole new means of marketing and distribution. It then moved into the manufacturing of appliances and tools under private labels, another innovation, then into a range of financial products and services—insurance, brokerage, credit cards—and later into telecommunications. While the company went through some hard times, it managed continually to regain its cutting edge, changing the definition of what it could do and be; despite category-killing competition from Wal-Mart and others, it remains a juggernaut in retailing today.

Or think about The Home Depot. Once the exclusive head-quarters for do-it-yourselfers, it finds itself in the early years of the twenty-first century confronting a changing market. It isn't only do-it-yourselfers shopping in the warehouse-sized Home Depot stores these days, it's people who very definitely don't want to do it themselves, but who instead want to choose their "look" and have someone else do all the work.

Seizing the opportunity of this new "audience," the huge company is quickly and nimbly reinventing itself. It now offers appliances, holiday products, fitness and recreational equipment, and consumer electronics products like digital cameras, home entertainment, even computers—not just the stuff for putting your home together or fixing it up, but the stuff you want inside your home as well.

There's nothing inherently radical about the innovations undertaken by The Home Depot and Sears, and neither enterprise is part of an industry considered cutting edge. Neither radical change nor revolutionary industry transformation is necessary. What *is* required is the ability consistently to escape from tradition and from hidebound notions of what "worked in the past" in order to reach out for new ideas, new processes, and new markets in a meaningful way.

MEET A "SERIAL INNOVATOR"

"I don't think the jobs are coming back," opines Luke Fields. "We need to find new ways to make money."

Fields backs his opinion with action. He is a forward-thinking, successful entrepreneur who knew he "never wanted to work for someone else." Instead, almost by default, he thought up a new way of making money. He succeeded so well, and so many times, he has become virtually a "serial innovator" who almost can't help himself from creating that next great business model. If he is not necessarily a pioneer or an absolute original—and by his own candid admission, he is not—he is nevertheless the guy who can put a new gloss on an old idea and make it pay. He has been doing so successfully for some time.

He started in college. Needing some extra cash, he came up with the idea of running a summer course designed for high school graduates who were about to go to college. As a "seasoned veteran" with two years of college under his belt, Luke was the main teacher as well as the entrepreneur, although he also recruited another soon-to-be-junior to help him instruct the soon-to-be-freshmen in everything they needed to know about making the transition to college.

The "course curriculum" included lessons on how to dress, a review of the best professors, a guide to fraternities that had the best parties, tips on what was cool—and what was decidedly uncool—and similar critical topics. "We made a few thousand bucks," says Luke. "We couldn't believe it! We repeated it for a couple of summers."

After graduation, Fields got a job selling magazine advertising in the Midwest. "It was a great job for a kid with a C-plus average. It didn't require much erudition or even intellect. It was a *relationship* business."

It was selling advertising that showed Fields he had a knack for building relationships—and for using that skill to build businesses. In fact, after a few years he and two friends bought the magazine—at that time still headquartered in Cincinnati. Now that he was in charge, Luke had another idea for growing the business: Publish more magazines. The core magazine served the packaging industry, but Luke had learned that the industry was complex, with different segments with different information needs.

The company's first new addition was a magazine for packaging suppliers. Next came an industry-specific magazine on mergers and acquisitions, then one on plastics, and another on packaging globally. Soon the company was publishing six different magazines and had moved its headquarters to Chicago, where many more packaging companies were located.

The publishing company thrived. With the packaging business virtually recessionproof, it did well even during the recession-laden 1970s. By the 1980s, however, Luke's two partners had pretty much lost interest. At just that time, a European company expressed interest in acquiring the business. "We thought of what might be a fair price for buying the business, and then doubled it," says Luke. "And they paid it!"

Part of the deal, however, was a noncompete clause for Luke; for five years, he was restricted from involvement in the magazine publishing business altogether.

Barred from publishing, Luke began a labeling company. His main aim in doing so was to find a way to subsidize his health insurance. Making good use of his enormous relationship skills, he turned the labeling business into a hit from the get-go. In due course, he parlayed some of the income from the labeling company to create a publication that was in fact a direct competitor to his initial packaging magazine. Adhering to the strict terms of his noncompete clause, he waited exactly five years before starting the competitive publication.

It too succeeded, and things were going along smoothly until personnel problems reared their ugly head. One of Luke's partners got together with a key salesperson in the labeling business to start their own labeling firm; their aim, in effect, was to try to steal some of Luke's hard-won customers. They didn't quite make it, but the Fields partnership ultimately broke apart—and along with it, some of the relationships among the former partners.

Fortunately, at the same time, Luke's new publishing business was taking off. Still loosely associated with the packaging world, Luke came up with two new topic innovations for his two magazines. He also started publishing online as well as in hard copy. "I don't want to be the innovator," says this serial entrepreneur; "I want to be number two." In other words, while Luke knows he is not a genius capable of totally original thought, he understands that he has a knack for putting a new spin on tired traditional notions.

He is also adamant about being on the cutting edge of technology—again, not as the creator of the new but as someone who takes best advantage of the new. It's why he spent big to get what is generally considered the best Web site in his industry. As a result, "people want to joint venture with us all the time," says Luke. And he adds: "I just play dumb and act like I don't get it."

An interesting postscript to the story: Some years ago, Luke began investing in real estate. No wonder he is well on his way to perpetual wealth.

Investing in the continually innovative enterprise means putting down stakes in something—not a stock or a bond or a financial instrument, but a product or service—that is representative of the future.

"INVESTING" IS A MATTER OF DEGREE

How do we define "investing" when it comes to continually innovative enterprises? The answer depends on the degree of your personal involvement. At the highest and riskiest level of personal involvement, you would essentially quit your current job and focus full time on the innovative enterprise. At the lowest level of personal involvement, you might invest in a limited partnership, private equity plan, or venture capital program in which the actual management of the enterprise—possibly even the choice of the enterprise to invest in—is beyond your reach and outside your control.

Between those two points lies a range of involvement from which you can choose the right level for yourself, depending on your interests, your willingness to spend time and effort and energy, and your ultimate commitment to the new venture. So the level of personal involvement is entirely up to you.

What we are certain of, however—what we can say without qualification or reservation—is that some degree of personal involvement is absolutely essential. Our research is unequivocal in this matter: Ninety percent of the income of those who today have achieved perpetual wealth comes from a business that is significantly controlled by the individual. Again, while the meaning of "significantly" in that sentence is open to interpretation, the fact of the involvement is not.

The reason is evident in the histories of today's perpetually wealthy—the heirs of progenitors who had the foresight to involve themselves in businesses that continue to produce income streams for their children, grandchildren, great-grandchildren and beyond. You don't have to go back too far in history to find such an example; it's evident in the story of Tom

Kramer, whom you met in Chapter 4. Two of the Kramer sons now also work in the excavation business Tom built. They are not just beneficiaries of the stream of wealth their father started; for both of them, the business is their concern and their career, and they will keep the wealth flowing into the next generation as well. The more involvement there is on the part of future generations, the more likely it is that the income stream will flow wide and fast; with diminishing personal involvement, the stream will eventually dry up.

But not everybody wants to work in the excavation business. Tom Kramer's middle son, for example, chose to start up his own entrepreneurial venture—and proved himself a chip off the old block and a natural businessman. In fact, not everybody wants to work in business at all, or sees himself or herself as suited to it, or has the interest or personality to get involved in a hands-on way.

No matter. If it isn't possible to change your personality, it also isn't necessary to change your career. There are many ways to invest in the continually innovative enterprise— all along that range of calibrated involvements—and to create a stream of wealth that can keep gushing for generations. All you have to do is search out, identify, understand, and seize opportunities.

RESEARCHING OPPORTUNITIES

As we stated at the outset of this chapter, opportunities are probably not going to fall into your lap. You'll have to go looking for them. Typically, you'll be looking for innovative enterprises in the embryo stage—innovations that haven't yet proven themselves but that need investment to do so. To be able to spot those innovations and identify them as opportunities, you'll need three things—time, research, and networking—and you'll need to apply all of them simultaneously.

Where do you start? At home—in your community, your neighborhood, by talking to your friends, and by thinking about what you already know and care about.

What needs are not being fulfilled in your community? Does your village need a coffee shop where folks can congregate after a workout at the local gym or before heading off to work or do chores? Do you get annoyed because you have to drive 30 miles to the nearest dry cleaner? Does everybody you know feel a similar annoyance, and if so, wouldn't it make sense to start a dry cleaning establishment right here? Living in a place is the best way to understand what that place needs in order to improve.

Once you've identified such a need, see if others feel as you do. Research the idea by talking to as many of your friends, neighbors, and acquaintances as you can. If it still makes sense, come up with a business model that might make sense in answering the need. Talk to others about investing with you. Above all, do your due diligence. Take the time, expend the research effort, and do the necessary networking.

Jennifer, a mother of three, is a manager at a large drug manufacturer. She lives in a nice home in a comfortable, affluent suburb. One day, after dropping her kids off at school, she got into a conversation with several other mothers; pretty quickly, the mothers were onto the subject of buying clothes for their kids, and all lamented that there were virtually no stores nearby that provided upscale children's clothing.

One of the mothers, Sue, had a retail background and confided to her friends that she would love to find some investors to back her in starting her own children's store in the area. Jennifer was interested. She asked around, talked up the idea, and discussed it with her lawyer husband. She also sought out the financial people at her company, took them to lunch, and asked what they thought. And she "researched" Sue, mostly by getting to know her, her background in retail, and the quality of her character.

Convinced that the idea was sound and that Sue was knowledgeable, honorable, and committed, Jennifer decided to provide substantial start-up capital for the business, which Sue would design, manage, and run. Today, Jennifer is benefiting handsomely from the success of the store. She is not hands-on in any way—Sue is absolutely in charge and does it all, reaping the greatest rewards—but Jennifer's annual portion of the profits is a substantial and growing part of her income stream.

Starting at home doesn't only mean finding a local need and creating a local solution. Your network of friends and acquaintances may be plugged into other opportunities beyond your immediate reach. To find out, ask. And listen. After all, you go to parties in your community, you socialize with others through your interests, and you meet and befriend the parents of your children's friends. What are people talking about? Even more to the point, what are others investing in that might spur you to get involved?

Ron is a contractor and a very conservative investor. A business owner who knows his own business well, Ron respects expert knowledge like his own, so he is inclined to follow his broker's advice—especially since the broker understands that Ron is risk averse. But Ron is also the product of a rural upbringing, and he has the Midwesterner's faith in the value of land as an investment. So when his accountant pointed out to him that he had no corporate pension or other source of ongo-ing income for his old age, Ron took some cash out of stocks and bonds and invested in farmland. He rented the land out to corn farmers who paid him an annual base amount plus a per-centage of their profits from the sale of their corn crop.

That's how Ron happened to hear about the ethanol plant going up in the next county—and about its need for investors. He set out to investigate the opportunity, calling on the experts who helped him in his business—his accountant, his lawyer, his broker. At the time, ethanol was something of an unknown quantity, so Ron also got in touch with some agronomists and soil scientists from the local agricultural commission to find out more about it.

Ron liked what he heard and made a substantial long-term investment in the plant. His investment grew steadily if in small increments for a while, but needless to say, it has gained dramatically over the last few years as the demand for ethanol has skyrocketed. In fact, Ron has scored a double win: He re-ceives an ongoing stream of income from the land rentals, and he is realizing a substantive long-term profit from his invest-ment in the ethanol plant. And it all happened because this conservative investor had his ears open to innovative opportu-nities and, despite the conservatism, wasn't afraid to take an educated, calculated risk.

ATTITUDE COUNTS

Conservative Ron's willingness to risk money on ethanol back in the day when most people probably thought "ethanol" might be a new headache medicine was perhaps not so surprising after all. We've looked into the different attitudes about wealth exhibited by those in career categories and the results are striking: Business owners, like Ron, are far more likely than professionals, real estate owners, or senior executives to view a down market as a buying opportunity and to take advantage of that opportunity. In fact, while only 30 percent to 40 percent of professionals, real estate owners, and senior executives look positively at a down market, an astonishing 58 percent of business owners do.

Business owners—along with real estate investors—also seem more optimistic about their financial futures than professionals or other wealthy individuals. More than 97 percent of business owners and real estate investors look past the bumps and blips in the economy to maintain a positive attitude about the future, compared to 85 percent of other affluent individuals.

Finally, when we ask people if their primary goal is to build wealth or to preserve wealth, 68 percent of real estate owners and 62 percent of business owners, no matter how old they are, assert that their primary goal is to build wealth.

So in buying nearby farmland and investing in an innovative ethanol venture, conservative Ron actually exhibited the optimism and forward vision that characterize business owners and real estate owners—two categories that combined most profitably in Ron himself.

THE IMPORTANCE OF NETWORKING

Ron's conservatism was the impetus for him to check with professionals—a sound idea when considering any investment. Where do you find them? Actually, you have a ready-made squadron of professionals you can tap—namely, your lawyer, broker, banker, accountant, and others you may have dealt with in the past.

If you think you don't "have" a lawyer, think again. Chances are you dealt with one when you closed on your house. You probably got a mortgage from the local bank, which means you have a banker you can call on. You likely have an accountant that does your taxes, and you almost certainly get a statement about your stock market portfolio from a broker several times a year. All of those people possess expertise you can draw on, and all of them are adept at putting together deals. In fact, the chances are that one or all of them are involved in putting together a deal right now. Who knows? It might be one you'd do well to be involved with.

Another way to take advantage of your network of friends, acquaintances, and local professionals is to let it be known that you are interested in investing in something. Put it out there: You're in the market for some sort of business venture, and you're ready to commit resources when the right one comes along. You will be surprised at how quickly and efficiently this grapevine works. You may get more responses than you bargained for, and although most will likely be nonstarters, there may be a few that will warrant further research and careful consideration. And there may eventually be the one that earns your interest and merits your involvement.

DON'T LET GEOGRAPHY STOP YOU

Of course, we are not recommending that you invest only in opportunities in your neighborhood or within driving distance of your home. The world is a village these days, and opportunities around the globe are and should be open to you. You can find them the same way you find local opportunities—by asking and listening and keeping your eyes and ears open, and by networking. The only thing that's different is the scope and size of the landscape upon which you do your looking and talking and listening.

Of course, it's always best to start with the Internet. In addition to searching for specific opportunities, be sure to check the Web sites of some brokerage firms like Schwab, E*TRADE, and Morgan Stanley, which often post far-flung investment opportunities for which they've created funds. In addition, if you deal with a private banker, ask him or her about private investment opportunities; at the very least, a private banker is likely to know how to access further information about such opportunities. And to be sure, you can also learn about distant opportunities from colleagues, acquaintances, and friends right in your own backyard.

Near or far, one good way to narrow the focus of your search is to concentrate on things you know and are passionate about. The lawyer who loved the track and bought a share in a promising thoroughbred colt . . . the garden-loving corporate executive who threw over corporate life to start her own nursery in a town that had none . . . the business owner in love with broadcasting who invested early in satellite radio . . . the theater-loving physician whose long-held wish to be an "angel" to a Broadway show finally came true—all these individuals involved themselves in what turned out to be solid investment opportunities by responding to the passions of their lives.

However you find out about the opportunity, and whatever the opportunity you identify, due diligence is essential, so be prepared to expend all the time, research effort, and networking necessary to assure yourself that this is indeed a commitment you want to undertake.

CALIBRATING YOUR LEVEL OF INVOLVEMENT

Once you have identified a continually innovative enterprise and have done your homework, how should you invest in it? Should you invest your time, engaging in running the operation in a hands-on manner? Should you invest your money only? To what extent?

The answers to these questions define your point of involvement along that spectrum between career change and putting money into a venture that someone else manages. Again, only you can decide on that level of involvement, and it will depend much more on your personality, desires, family, other responsibilities, checkbook, and personal style than on any scientific measure. To help you, however, we've compiled a list of investment options.

FRANCHISES

The franchise is a perfectly legitimate way to enter a business, industry, or marketplace, and franchise opportunities abound.

Let's be clear about what a franchise is: A business owner (the franchisor) licenses individuals like you (the franchisee) to operate outlets of the franchisor's business. Franchisors may offer a product franchise (as in running a car dealership) or a business format franchise (like a fast-food or motel chain). The franchisee follows the business model of the franchisor and uses the franchisor's property, trademarks, and trade names.

Unless you are buying just a share of a franchise, this tends to be a very hands-on level of involvement, and it is often very hard work. There is also, of course, the substantial up-front purchase price of the franchise license, and there may be other costs as well. Thanks to a fair amount of early abuses in franchising, the industry is now highly regulated on both the federal and the state level, so be very careful that you are getting all the rights and privileges guaranteed to franchisees by law. Check out the Internet not just for franchising opportunities but for franchise brokers and consultants, and lawyers and bankers who specialize in franchising.

Our view of franchising? It is a limited and slightly limiting way of investing in a continually innovative enterprise, but if done carefully, it may prove to be an effective entry into the world of investing in an innovative enterprise.

PARTNERSHIPS, PRIVATE EQUITY, VENTURE CAPITAL

General partnerships, limited partnerships, and syndicates all define investments involving multiple investors who pool their resources or share ownership in an investment, property, or company, and all three terms define legal distinctions. In a general partnership, all the investors are equally liable for all debts and legal actions and all share equally in the management and control of the company or investment. Limited partners have limited liability—and limited potential rewards. Syndicates may set their own rules for how the partnership will work.

Private equity opportunities represent a chance to invest in assets that are not traded publicly—that is, they are not available on the stock market. Private equity funds are typically created by private equity firms for the purpose of investing in companies targeted as potentially rewarding. These funds control the management of the target companies in which they invest, so it is not a blind or remote investment. It is, however, typically a very high-priced investment requiring a very substantial minimum "entry fee."

The same is true for venture capital investments—which are pooled investments that finance a new business, preferably the kind of continually innovative enterprise that can put its investors on track to perpetual wealth. Venture capital investments are typically very high-risk, but they offer potentially high returns. They have historically been associated with technological innovations that, when successful, have helped to reshape our culture and economy.

Your banker or broker will likely be able to educate you on any and all of these types of investments, where you can get more information, and on the specifics of actual investments. You can and should search online as well.

HOMEWORK ALERT

As with any investment in continually innovative enterprises—in fact, as with any investment—you need to do your homework before you sign on the dotted line or write the check. Any pooled investment venture in which you become involved needs an airtight contract that clearly identifies the obligations of all the parties and that clearly spells out what happens in the event the venture fails.

We've heard lots of horror stories about what can happen if the contract isn't clear or airtight. There was the investor who invested in an instant-photo shop and received only a receipt for the amount he invested. When the shop went belly-up a year later and the investor wanted to sell both the empty storefront and all the equipment inside, he found he had no rights whatsoever to do so. The whole venture was, for him, a costly write-off.

You also need to do some due diligence on the other partners or participants in your pooled investment, and you should monitor the project or business by scrutinizing the company's statements and other available business documents. We know an individual who was presented with a great opportunity to invest in a lithium plant in Russia during the 1990s. He checked out the opportunity pretty thoroughly, decided it had great financial potential, and invested a significant amount of money. But he really did not know the individual running the plant in

Russia and, since he spoke no Russian and was 8,000 miles away, he also had no good way to track how the business was doing. What's more, despite a seemingly sound contract, bringing a legal case against a Russian citizen in Russia—again, from an 8,000-mile distance—seemed an unlikely, messy, losing proposition under the best of circumstances.

In the end, this particular investor was able to recover his initial investment, but the only gain he realized was a valuable lesson in how not to invest—plus a lot of aggravation and worry.

The bottom line? Time, effort, and energy spent in doing due diligence before the fact can save time, effort, energy, and money after the fact. In any pooled investment or partnership, make sure you know what is at stake and with whom you are dealing. Then create a written agreement that details the terms and conditions of participation clearly and in a way that ensures your interests will be protected.

Anything short of crystal clarity and complete protection of your interests and rights could prove to be a costly detour or worse on your progress toward getting rich at all, much less staying rich enough to be able to pass it on.

A PORTRAIT OF PERPETUAL WEALTH: THE HARD-WORKING ENTREPRENEUR

Sally Brown was widowed when she was in her early fifties. It was not totally unexpected, but it was nevertheless devastating. "We married young, but Jim always had health issues," Sally explains, gazing out the window of her comfortable country home. Slender, fit, and normally enthusiastic, Sally admits to feeling her loss afresh every day.

Jim was initially diagnosed with cancer at twenty-seven. He endured cobalt therapy, chemotherapy, and other treatments—much harsher back then than their equivalents today—and over the years suffered various cancer relapses as well as recurring cardiac problems. He died during a relatively routine heart bypass operation. Difficult as his struggle was, Jim's ill health "really brought us together," says Sally. "We knew we had each other."

They did everything together. Both seemed born entrepreneurs, and the initiative of one seemed to trigger an equal initiative on the other's part. Jim had grown up in the Midwest and had an interest in the cattle business. He and Sally moved to Montana for a time, where Jim made himself an expert in the Simmental breed of cattle, which was not then well known in the Midwest. With the help of an expert breeder, he introduced the Simmental to his home region. The move was highly successful, growing in value not only through sales of the cattle but especially for the semen that was frozen and sold.

The Browns didn't stop there. "Jim was very good at what he did," says Sally, "but the cattle business always had its ups and downs." To add some stability to their financial picture, Sally and Jim decided to take some of their earnings from the cattle business and invest in real estate. They bought a couple of buildings in the downtown area of the small town in which they lived. At the same time, Sally decided to open up a Western store in one of the buildings. The store, specializing in jeans, cowboy boots, cowboy hats, and other regalia, caught the crest of a wave of popularity for all things "country" and rode it to stunning success.

But the retail business also has its ups and downs, and Sally's cowboy store burned down after a few years in business. Sally sold out the inventory, rebuilt the building, and used it as rental property. When Sally and Jim finally sold their downtown buildings, they realized many times their initial investment. Sally has since used some of the proceeds of that yield to invest in other real estate.

Still not willing to relax her entrepreneurial drive, and always worried about the vagaries of the cattle business, Sally decided to try her hand at selling baskets. Her seeming knack for moving with the times and spotting the latest trends again served her well. This time, the trend was basket sales parties held in individual homes—like the early Tupperware parties.

Sally dove in, quickly became the top-selling salesperson for the manufacturer, and has continued to hold that title for almost 18 years. "It's really just about taking care of my customers," she says diffidently, "doing special things for each of them so they know they are appreciated, and giving them good ideas." She continues her highly hands-on involvement in the basket business, routinely coming up with new ideas for products and marketing that keep the business on the cutting edge at all times.

At the same time, she keeps a firm hand on the management of her real estate, managing her rental properties and parlaying her original investments to make new purchases.

Jim's death was gut wrenching, of course. In addition to her grief, Sally confronted the high-stress challenge of unwinding his business and financial interests. "The cattle business is a complicated business," she says. "When Jim died, it was just after September 11, 2001. I knew that I couldn't sell all of the cattle at that time; the prices were really low. But I also knew that I didn't know how to take care of them. In addition, knowing how and where to most profitably sell the semen is a really specialized process."

She turned to Jim's former business partners and associates to help her with the eventual sale of the cattle. Although she was aware that "I probably didn't make as much as Jim eventually would have," she also knew that the burden of owning the cattle—an area in which she had never become expert—had its costs as well. At the same time, Sally held onto some of the frozen semen; ever the entrepreneur, she sees it as a valuable investment that she will sell at the appropriate time.

Jim's death also triggered phone calls from a number of brokers eager to serve as financial advisors to this wealthy widow, but Sally does not feel comfortable relying on strangers for advice. Like many small business owners, she thinks of her attorney and her accountant as her primary advisors, and she looks to her son-in-law for advice on her investments.

Although she knows she is financially sound and even fortunate, Sally continues to worry about the future. The country house is expensive to maintain, but she is not yet ready to give it up: too many memories. She also worries about "something happening" that might make it difficult or impossible for her to take care of herself. "I worry about being sick and not being able to do my business," she says.

"I don't live in a world where I think everything will be perfect because it won't," says this savvy realist. "All that Jim and I went through has made me grow. We lived to enjoy what we worked for. We were very close, and we were each other's cheerleader. I will miss that, but I will work it out."

"Working it out" may indeed be Sally Brown's greatest strength—and the reason why she is creating a sustainable fortune that can offer wealth to her heirs for many generations to come. She has consistently seized the opportunity in each changing circumstance of her life. She started with nothing, undertook innovative enterprises that engaged her interest, sold them, and then moved on to new initiatives.

At the time of Jim's death, she wisely sold the riskier venture that had been his enterprise but kept the real estate. In her midfifties, she is still entrepreneurial. Perhaps because she has seen personal loss, she is determined to create a bulwark against financial loss. And while the ongoing income stream from her sales prowess allows her to live a comfortable life, it is her continuing involvement in innovations and new initiatives as well as her investment in real estate that are providing her a foundation, whether she knows it or not, for perpetual wealth.

CHAPTER 7

WRITING YOUR PERPETUAL WEALTH PRESCRIPTION

You now have a pretty good idea of how the perpetually rich get that way. You've had a thorough grounding in the concept. You understand that while there are many ways to become rich—even very rich—there are two essentials for gaining the kind of wealth that can keep you comfortably rich throughout your lifetime and the lifetime of your heirs.

1. **Buying real estate:** putting your assets in properties that produce an income stream and that themselves can be passed on as part of a legacy.

2. **Engaging in continually innovative entrepreneurship:** creating, developing, directing, or in some way being involved in a company, product, or service that grows by persistently refreshing or reinventing itself.

You may indeed make your fortune in the stock market, or perhaps you're just someone who works hard enough and smart enough at something to make a good living at it. Whatever the source of your assets, you can make them grow beyond your expectations and last well beyond your lifetime if you also invest in real estate and innovative enterprises.

You've learned the pretty simple reason behind this truth: that real estate and continually innovative entrepreneurship act as the twin engines of a perpetual-motion income stream machine. They churn more assets for you to feed to other investments, and they do so to the rhythm of their own economic cycles. If the stock market should falter—or worse, if it should crash—real estate and the innovative enterprise endure.

Even investors who have lost their shirts on Wall Street still need a place to live, and they'll still find a way to pay rent. By the same token, an innovative enterprise in its early days of development—before the business goes public—will likely be insulated from the vagaries of the market.

Moreover, innovative enterprises are driven more by what we might term "life needs" than by the gyrations of the financial markets. Suppose your enterprise is a café that attracts a squad of breakfast regulars. Chances are good they'll still need to chow down even if the market tumbles. In fact, your café could well become the place where people gather to talk about the crash and comfort one another over lost savings.

Another relevant example: Let's say your business produces high-end, kitschy socks. A stock market crash might make consumers think twice about buying fancy socks, and they will likely buy socks less often than they once did, but it won't keep them from buying socks altogether. The likelihood is that your product will sell in lower volume and you may have to lower the price, but people are still going to need socks—no matter what happens on the U.S. stock exchanges and around the world.

Of course, we are not saying that a major stock market crash won't affect the value of real estate and the prospects of an innovative enterprise. It may indeed. A business enterprise specifically related to the market—for example, a business within the financial industry, or an entity that services that industry—may well swoon along with the market.

Moreover, a market crash will typically depress the economy as a whole, and if that happens, the business enterprise in which you're engaged—just about any business enterprise, for that matter—will feel the sting. Even without an external, sweeping event like a market crash, any and all businesses suffer glitches and weather downturns; that's just the price of admission in running any business.

Nevertheless, the enterprise that can continue to reinvent itself is, like real estate, a long-term source of income stream. While both real estate and business cycles may oscillate, they will typically do so in different ways and at different times from the zigs and zags or leaps and dips of the capital markets. In financial terms, they offer a hedge against those markets. Most important, they do so by providing income and enhancing equity.

But understanding how perpetual wealth works is one thing; putting it into action can be quite another. How do you turn the behavior of others into a prescription for yourself? How do you build your own model for perpetual wealth—a plan of action for your lifetime and a paradigm that future generations, who will benefit from your plan of action, can also follow?

You do it pretty much the way you do anything else: one step at a time.

KEEP IT IN CONTEXT

Back in Chapter 3, you identified the difference between the way you allocate your assets today and the way assets are allocated in the benchmark model. You looked at both dollar value and percentages and compared where you stand vis-à-vis the benchmark model. Let's bring some of that data forward now

MY INVESTMENTS	DOLLAR VALUE OF MY INVESTMENTS	BENCHMARK PERCENTAGE OF TOTAL HOUSEHOLD ASSETS	MY PERCENT-AGE OF TOTAL HOUSEHOLD ASSETS
MARKETABLE SECURITIES	35–45		
• Cash and short-term securities	5–7		
• Stocks, bonds, and mutual funds	30–40		
• Alternatives, including hedge funds, venture capital, private equity	4–5		
• Other investment products, including unit investment trusts, 529s, and the like	3–4		
PRIVATELY HELD BUSINESSES (CONTINU-ALLY INNOVATIVE ENTERPRISES)	25–35		
REAL ESTATE	23–29		
• Equity in principal residence	11–13		
• Income-producing property	3–6		
• Second home	5–7		
• Other real estate	3–5		
• Undeveloped land	2–4		
• Third/additional residences	2–4		
LIFE INSURANCE AND ANNUITIES	5–7		
RETIREMENT PLAN	3–5		
OTHER INVESTMENTS	3–5		

to create an overall picture of where you are and where you're hoping to go. Refer to the dollar values and percentage allocations in the chart on page 47 and reinsert them here.

This is the context in which you'll start creating your own model to get rich, stay rich, and pass it on. It's the big-picture view of your personal version of money forever. You can see what you're aiming for (the benchmark percentages) and you can see how far you have to go (the difference between your current percentage and the benchmark percentage). Keep this context front and center as you work through the exercises of this chapter.

It's now time to start writing your personal prescription for perpetual wealth. That's exactly what this chapter is about. We've divided it into two parts corresponding to the two secrets of perpetual wealth: getting engaged in real estate and investing in the continually innovative enterprise. In each part, we've set forth a sequence of steps for you to follow—along with some charts and worksheets to help you execute the steps.

Think of the chapter as your very own workbook, the place where you lay out a clear road map you can follow. The deliverable at the end of the chapter, once you've completed the workbook part, will be the building blocks for your personal wealth prescription. We've also added a quick summary checklist at the end of the chapter.

It all starts with real estate.

PART 1: GETTING INTO REAL ESTATE

There are two essential preliminary steps to take before perusing the Properties Available listings in the newspaper. These include a number of issues to keep in mind as you begin to consider properties, and some key assessments to make once you think you've found a property to invest in.

Step 1. How Much Do You Have to Invest?

The very first necessity is to determine how much capital you have available to put into real estate. The table on page 129 shows the typical sources of capital available to most people. To complete the table, refer back to the chart you've just created and bring forward the number representing the total equity in your real estate investments. Make sure that you have subtracted from the market value of the real estate the amount of any mortgage, home equity loan, or other real estate pledge. Enter this amount in the first field.

Now bring forward the dollar value of your marketable securities—an obvious source of capital—and of other investments against which you might borrow. Fill in the value of your privately held business, if there is one, and bring forward also the cash value of your insurance policy; some policies allow you to borrow against the cash value.

The total is the maximum source of capital you can consider for a down payment. Consider it carefully, however. It is probably not prudent to put all of this down right now; you may want to hold some capital for other purposes and liquidate only a portion of your investments toward the down payment.

SOURCE OF CAPITAL	DOLLAR AMOUNT
Equity in your primary residence or other real estate	$_____
Marketable securities	$_____
Other investments	$_____
Privately held business	$_____
Cash value of life insurance	$_____
TOTAL	$_____

You might also think about pledging a percentage of your marketable securities as collateral for a loan for the down payment or even for the entire purchase amount.

You might also choose to take out a home equity loan on your primary residence or borrow from your 401(k) plan to get the funds for a down payment for this important investment. Be sure you understand the related financing and payment obligations, and recognize that if you borrow from your 401(k) account, those assets will not be there for retirement (unless the sum is repaid) and obviously will not continue to grow.

Revisit your risk tolerance profile—from page 63 in Chapter 4—before you borrow against current assets for the down payment *and* secure a loan for the remaining value of your real estate investment. Prudence should always prevail.

However you arrive at the amount you are willing to spend to get into real estate—and however you put together the amount—that is your projected down payment on an initial investment property.

The down payment rule of thumb for investment properties is 20 percent to 25 percent of the total purchase price. So the next step is to calculate the putative purchase price you can handle given your projected down payment. Give yourself a range of properties to consider:

> If my projected down payment is 20 percent of the purchase price, the purchase price will be $_____. That is the bottom of the range.

> If my projected down payment is 25 percent of the purchase price, the purchase price will be $_____. That is the top of the range.

You now know the maximum price you can pay for properties in which to invest.

Step 2. Can You Get Financing?

Check with a mortgage lender to ascertain the amount and kind of loan for which you can qualify. The answer will be based partly on the amount of your projected down payment but also on your overall credit rating, including the payment history on the mortgage of your primary residence and, more important, how your overall personal financial profile looks to the lender—particularly your net worth, calculated by your assets minus your liabilities.

Step 3. Start Looking—With Objective Eyes.

Armed with your projected down payment and an answer from your mortgage lender, you're in a good position to start looking for the right investment property. You've got a range of prices to guide you, and you've got a near assurance that, once you've found the right piece of real estate, you'll qualify for financing.

But there are a few things you should know as you go forward about *how* to look for the right property.

There is a distinct difference between real estate as an investment and real estate as a place in which to live or work. You're very likely familiar with the latter, so it's important to understand that the former is entirely different. After all, when you go out looking for a home or workplace for yourself, you respond to highly subjective criteria and are driven by emotions having to do with comfort, aesthetics, and other qualities difficult to articulate, much less define. Certainly you want the rental property you buy to be attractive to potential renters, and you as a buyer will certainly have some subjective responses to a property, but what you are buying is an investment, and there are some important factors you need to be aware of before you get swept away by subjective responses.

We've drawn up a list of some of those factors, categorized by the type of property you'll be looking at. It's important to pay close attention to both the strengths of the potential investment and its challenges. Above all, don't let yourself fall in love with a property, and do remember the three great fundamentals of buying real estate: location, location, location.

Step 4. Found a Property? Ask Some Caution Questions.

You've found a property that seems right. The price is within your range and appears to be a sound choice given the objective realities of this type of an investment.

It's time for what we call the "caution questions." The caution questions you would pose as a home buyer (or as someone buying a place to work) would be of a very different character, so we've compiled a list of the key caution questions you need to ask yourself when considering a property for investment.

PROPERTY TYPE	STRENGTHS	CHALLENGES
• Single-family residence	• Usually lowest cost of entry • Easiest to manage	• Often longer time frame to make a profit on investment • Works most effectively if investor is personally able to provide some of the maintenance • Must choose an area in which it is routine to rent out single-family homes
• Multifamily residence or condominium	• Can pay for itself quickly	• Usually requires larger up-front investment depending on the number of units you are considering and what percentage of the building you will own • Must make sure that you have qualified renters and must collect rents • Need to ensure current rent (if existing unit) is competitive with (or maybe slightly below) market levels • Generally higher maintenance costs • May need to have management company involved
• Commercial real estate	• Greater ability to pass expenses back to tenant • Generally longer-term lease arrangements	• Strength of tenant's business is critical • Build-out may be more expensive to attract tenants • Management can be time consuming • Need to continually be aware of any changes in zoning, taxes, etc., within community
• Undeveloped land	• Great opportunity for return if chosen in correct location	• Largest carrying cost: real estate taxes (earns no income) • Riskiest if wrong location • May have to hold for longest period of time • Need continually to be aware of any changes in zoning, taxes, etc., within community

If you're considering a single-family residence:

• Is the location appropriate for rental? To answer this, find out if there are other homes in the area that are rented—or if this is a high-end area in which most families purchase homes and families only rent homes on a short-term basis.

> ➤ If the area has a large pool of rentals, chances are good you'll easily find tenants; this is clearly a place where people look for rentals and clearly feel comfortable renting.

> ➤ A low pool of renters, by contrast, may only mean that your rental in the midst of all these owned homes could be a very attractive prospect indeed. That's something to keep in mind in marketing the house. Also keep in mind that companies or other organizations may move people into an area for "temporary" assignments of one, two, or three years; those workers may well be interested in a rental rather than in buying, so you might want to alert the human resources departments of local companies that you have a prize property in a prize area available for rent.

> ➤ Other short-term renters may be renovating their homes or may have just moved into the area and want to explore the situation for six months or a year before they buy their own home. In such a case, the paucity of rental properties may simply mean there's little competition and you can charge a premium rent.

- Are there businesses in the area that employ individuals who are unable to afford to purchase homes?

  ➤ If so, it's a likely rental area.

- How much will you need to expend on improvements to make the property attractive enough to rent? Is it a matter of a coat of paint and a few plants out front, or are new bathrooms, a renovated kitchen, and major structural work required?

  ➤ Estimate the expenses and when they will be required.

- Is there currently a tenant? What is the monthly rent? What is the length of the current tenant's lease?

  ➤ You want to know how long it will be before you can raise the rent, if desirable. Also, if the rent is maxed out, you want to know from a competitive perspective how long you're locked into that high income—that is, how long the lease is. If it's up for renewal soon, the next lease may be at the current rate because an increase may price the property out of the market.

- How much are the real estate taxes on the property? What is the schedule of assessments or tax revaluation?

  ➤ You need to know what you're going to be paying in the future.

- Has the property been subjected to any significant flooding? When was the roof most recently replaced? Other maintenance issues?

➤ You're determining if what you're buying is a sound structure.

If you're looking at a multifamily residence:

• What are the details of all existing leases: amount of rent being charged, length of each lease, provisions of the leases?

➤ You want to know how much longer you are legally bound by the current leases. If the rents are now below market, this will tell you how long you must wait before you increase your income. If the rates are above market, this may detract from the property's attractiveness to prospective tenants.

• Are other rents in the area comparable to those being charged for the property under consideration? Notably higher? Notably lower?

➤ This will let you know if you may have to lower rents to attract tenants, or, by contrast, if you can raise rents and still be competitive.

• What are the facts of the area's housing plant? Does the community have a real need for rental units?

➤ Just because a property is available does not necessarily make it attractive. If houses are standing empty and no one is moving into this community, look elsewhere.

• What is the age of the building, and how does it compare to others in the area?

➤ Maintenance is one issue. In addition, an older building in a community containing lots of new, high-function buildings may be unattractive. On the other hand, this may be an opportunity to invest in some improvements while keeping the "old" appearance so as to market the units as "classic," offering a style of living that harks back to a more gracious time while offering all the modern conveniences.

• Are any new housing developments planned in the area?

➤ If so, are people going to gravitate there instead of to your multifamily residence?

• How old are the current tenants? What is the turnover rate in the building?

➤ The rule of thumb is that the best rental tenant is a seventy-year-old widow: She pays the rent regularly, has a very soft footprint (i.e., does virtually no damage), and will never move. By contrast, newly married couples and young single people tend not only to move on quickly, they also may feel less of a stake in the building and its well-being.

• When was the last real estate assessment? What are the current taxes?

➤ Again, it's essential to know what the real estate tax picture is, both now and for the future.

- How much will it cost to update or upgrade the building? What is the condition of the roof? Furnaces? Other?

  ➤ Soundness of structure and plant is key; you want to know if your rental income will be consumed two years from now by the need to put on a new roof.

When considering commercial properties:

- Do you understand the income stream? What about related expenses like snow plowing, parking lot maintenance, fees and permits, other issues?

  ➤ Commercial *is* different. Give yourself a crash course in leases, operations, and facilities management.

- Have you reviewed the terms of all existing leases? How long are the leases?

  ➤ Again, the point is to know the limits under which you'll be operating and the possibilities available.

- What types of businesses are in the property? How long have they been there? How well established are the businesses?

  ➤ Stability is of course desirable; fly-by-night "gimmick" companies as tenants can fade as quickly as they appeared. Safety and security are also concerns; a company that mixes volatile chemicals in the basement may not be your favorite tenant. Best are companies with a stake in the area, a record of stability, and a long-term future.

• What would be the cost to upgrade the building or to make needed repairs or renovations? What about the cost of desired renovations?

> You want to know what it will take to make the "product" marketable and competitive.

• What expenses are covered by tenants?

> Again, commercial is different. Be sure you know where tenants' responsibilities end and yours begin.

If you're thinking about investing in undeveloped land:

• What are the taxes on the property, and what is the cost of insurance?

> Simply put, you want to know precisely what your operating expense or carrying costs will be.

• How is the property currently zoned? If the zoning is not favorable for development, what will it take in this community to get a zoning change so you can build something of value on the property?

> This may require a political as well as a financial answer. Be sure you understand where the centers of power lie and what the issues are.

- How much other undeveloped land is there in the community or area?

> ➤ This will tell you how valuable your land will be in 20 years. The goal is to be the only game in town—or one of the few games in town, in any event.

Step 5. Figure Out the Economics.

The fundamental facts of the purchase deal plus the answers to your caution questions should be sufficient preparation for understanding the economics of investing in the particular property under consideration. The aim is to figure out if buying the property is going to provide positive cash flow. In other words, is this property worth it?

We use cash flow to analyze the investment because cash flow is really what this is all about. We're talking about the cash a property generates for you out of the revenues it brings in after expenses have been paid: liquid income, or ready cash you can use to buy more properties or enlarge your investments in some other manner.

A cash flow analysis is a pretty simple document. It states your operating cash flow in, your operating expenses out, and the change left over when you've subtracted expenses out from cash in. To figure out whether the property under consideration is going to provide you a cash flow that is worth the purchase price—and the effort—use the template here.

Start by developing a complete monthly cash flow analysis for the first year. Note the actual income, unit by unit, that the property yields today. But year one isn't enough; you need to project the cash flow three years out and five years out, so you

PROJECTED CASH FLOW ANALYSIS

Revenues	Months 1–6	Months 7–12	Year 1	Year 2	Year 3	Year 4	Year 5
Rental Income							
(Expected Vacancy)	( )	( )	( )	( )	( )	( )	( )
Other Income							
Total Net Revenues							
Expenses							
Utilities							
Electricity							
Water/Sewer/Garbage							
Gas							
Cable							
Assessments							
Insurance							
Maintenance							
Debt Servicing							
Total Expenses							
Cash Flow Before Tax Benefits							
Tax Benefits							
Net Anticipated Cash Flow							

will need to estimate income shifts for years two, three, four, and five. Review each of your tenants' leases to determine when any rent increase is scheduled and when the lease expires. The hope is that a new lease will enable you to increase the monthly rent. Complete this unit-by-unit assessment for the first five years of your possible ownership of the property.

You will also need to ascertain the historical vacancy rate of the property as a percentage of the total annual rent. Obviously, vacancies mean no income, so adjust your cash flow analysis, both current and projected, accordingly. How should you figure vacancy rates? They tend to differ from property type to property type. For a commercial property, the rule of thumb is an annual vacancy rate of 5 percent. On a single-unit property—a single-family home, for example—where it may take you two to three months to rent the property, the vacancy could mean as much as 15 percent to 20 percent of your annual rent, so a vacancy on a single-unit property can put a substantial dent in your earning potential.

The field labeled "Other Income" in the cash flow analysis template might encompass a large range of items, from the laundry room machines to passing on the costs of cable TV in your leases. Anything else on the property that brings you any sort of income should be included here.

This isn't so hard to figure, is it? Indeed, income is fairly easy to project. The expense side of the ledger is a bit tougher, especially because operating expenses tend not to occur in specified amounts or to follow a regular schedule like rents.

What constitutes the operating expenses of a real estate property? First you must figure the normal, obvious costs of insurance, taxes, utilities like landscaping and snow removal, and annual maintenance—that is, the routine, expected upkeep of the property. Property maintenance tends to follow a fairly regular schedule. Just as you replace the water filters in your own house every three months, repair the gutters in the summer, and typically get the whole thing repainted every five years, there will be—should be—a checklist of routine maintenance for the rental property under consideration, so these "regular" maintenance costs must be factored in.

In addition, if you're buying one or more units in a condominium or a cooperative association, you will typically have to pay monthly assessments to the association that operates the condo or co-op or—yes, there is such a thing—the condop. On occasion, these associations also impose special assessments for special purposes. Obviously, all need to be factored into your analysis as well.

So, as you did on the income side, start with monthly estimates of these operating expenses for the first year, then use these figures to project out on a three-year to five-year basis.

There is another important item that you'll need to add to the cash flow analysis—namely, some kind of backup money for emergency repairs. If you own your own home, you already know that you have to expect the unexpected to happen—and you'd better be prepared for it. Where rental property is concerned, you prepare for the unexpected with what is universally called a "rainy day fund," although the technical term is a reserve account. This is money you hold back for the day the sewer connection under the building parking lot breaks and you arrive to find a sinkhole in front of your income-producing rental property. It happens.

How much should you keep back in the rainy day fund? Much like the vacancy projection, determining the appropriate level of reserve is a property-by-property estimate—even an investor-by-investor estimate. If you have invested in a large property in partnership with multiple other investors, you will be able to make what's called a "capital call" to them asking for additional capital. In this case, you may not need to have a reserve.

But if you're in this investment alone, the amount of the rainy day fund will depend on how much reserve you have left after you've paid the down payment for the property. If you are fairly well leveraged, then a good rule of thumb might be to keep 5 percent to 10 percent of your annual income from the property in reserve. Whatever percentage you decide upon, you'll have to estimate the rainy day fund monthly for the first year and annually thereafter. However much you keep in reserve, invest your rainy day funds in conservative short-term vehicles that you can quickly liquidate when—surprise!—you drive up to the edge of the sinkhole.

There's one more set of expenses to add to the cash flow analysis mix: debt service expenses. What is it costing you to finance the building's purchase? Again, estimate these costs for the first year, the first three years, and the first five, and write those numbers into the appropriate fields.

Now let's see what the cash flow analysis tells us. Look at your net anticipated cash flow for the first year, the first three years, and the first five years. Is the cash flow positive in each of these periods? By "positive," we mean: Is the property self-sustaining? The opposite, a negative cash flow, would be a property that draws down on your personal finances—not a desirable end at all.

If the property is not showing a positive cash flow for any of these periods, why not? Is the rent below market rates and locked in for many years to come? Perhaps the cost of servicing your debt is too high relative to the property's purchase price and rental income. Whatever the reason, a negative cash flow anywhere in your analysis is a red flag. You may want to consider renegotiating the purchase price to make the cash flow economics work. You may also want to ask yourself what the prospects are for above-market-rate appreciation. But keep in mind that a negative cash flow may force you to sell the property long before this hoped-for appreciation ever comes to pass.

If the cash flow analysis comes up positive across this chart, however, you're almost surely looking at a sound investment that can be a reliable source of cash income.

The cash flow stream from the property is not its only benefit, however. Talk to your accountant about factoring in the tax-related benefits of owning this type of real estate. Such benefits may include local and state tax incentives as well as the after-tax impact of depreciation allowance, which can amount to a significant annual tax savings. Exactly what benefits you can expect will depend entirely on your local laws, and the differences can make for very different impacts on your cash flow.

Once you've done the cash flow analysis, however, you'll have all the information you need to determine whether this is the right "starter" property for getting into real estate. If it is, buy it—and congratulate yourself on your purchase. If it isn't, there are plenty more properties where that one came from, so keep looking until the right one comes along.

Always keep in mind the big picture: You are doing this in an attempt to close the gap between your current asset allocation model and the benchmark asset allocation model of the perpetually wealthy. Getting into real estate is an essential part of the model but it is equally important that you do it right. So follow the steps carefully. Be realistic. Stay objective. And don't delay.

A PORTRAIT OF PERPETUAL WEALTH:
MONEY YOU CAN SEE

Debbie Simpson is the proud mother of two children. She began her career as a hair stylist and is now a stay-at-home mom. Debbie enjoys collecting antiques and looks especially for old martini shakers, furniture, and perfume bottles. Her real specialty, however, is investing in real estate.

Gaining expertise in real estate may seem a quintessentially Southern California thing to do, but Debbie was anything but an expert when she and her husband, John, began to compile their real estate portfolio. They were able to make their first investment only because they took out a home equity loan on their house. That first property was a beat-up old bungalow a few blocks from the beach. Debbie and John fixed it up themselves, sold it for a profit, and used the profit to buy a building with multiple rental units.

That became the pattern: Debbie would spot an old property for them to buy, John would spearhead a first-class renovation, and they would either sell the property or rent it out for income. In time, this cycle of continually investing, rehabbing, and selling gave the Simpsons a significant amount of real estate throughout Southern California—a good deal of it in the highly desirable Venice Beach area. John is now the full-time manager of their real estate portfolio while Debbie stays home with the kids (although she still keeps an eye out for the right kind of property).

The Simpsons have experienced some financial downturns—although not from real estate. They lost a significant amount of money in the bear market that followed September 11, 2001, and while they're determined to invest in stocks again some day, it probably won't be soon. "That's money we will never see again," Debbie says of the losses on Wall Street. "At least with real estate, we can see it. It doesn't just go away."

Still, Debbie feels that she and John may be overallocated in real estate, and she thinks about selling some of their properties in order to invest in other areas. The Simpsons have created trusts for their children and have no worries about being able to maintain their lifestyle, travel, or buy anything they'd like. The reason? That significant monthly income from rentals. Besides, says Debbie, "If things ever got tight, I could sell one of the properties."

These native Californians feel no need to get up and go elsewhere. They love their house on the beach and hope to stay there for the rest of their lives. They know they have created all the security for themselves and their children that money can buy. They are engaged in the life of their community and are particularly involved with a homeless shelter for teens. But as Debbie says, they can do all this because they have what their real estate investments provide: "cash in the bank."

PART 2:
INVESTING IN THE CONTINUALLY INNOVATIVE ENTERPRISE

Back in Chapter 4, you assessed your own personal tolerance for risk. It might be wise to refer back to that self-assessment, because the first question you need to ask before investing in a continually innovative enterprise is whether you're willing to take the risk on a venture of your own creation or would you prefer to invest in someone else's. This is a "life" question, and only you can answer it.

For the record, we should add that there is no value judgment placed on either of these alternatives. One choice—between an enterprise that you develop personally and someone else's enterprise idea—is not better than the other. Nor does one choice demonstrate a tougher spine than the other, or more moral fiber, or even a more exciting personality. And there is no guarantee of success when investing in either your own idea or someone else's; these are equal-opportunity risks. So make the choice based on your personal situation and your personal preferences—nothing else.

Step 1. Search Out Opportunities

How will you find the enterprise that can put you on the path to perpetual wealth? One way is to look for opportunities that are in search of investors. Opportunities like this exist just about everywhere, which is why you must constantly search them out and be aggressive in asking about new ventures and asserting your interest in investing.

One thing is pretty certain: There are more enterprises in

search of investors than there are investors in search of enterprises. And one of the simplest ways to find the right opportunity is to shake the trees a little. There are four main ways to do that.

Check with Friends and Family

Start in your own backyard—with your family, friends, and acquaintances. Maybe you overheard people talking about an investment opportunity at a recent cocktail party. Maybe a fellow commuter mentioned something about a start-up company she thought showed promise. Maybe the guy in the next cubicle at work keeps arguing with his brother-in-law over the phone, claiming he simply doesn't have "that kind of money to invest." What are they all talking about? Ask them.

Or perhaps you've heard or overheard nothing at all. In that case, it's up to you to start the conversation. First, make a list of likely friends and family members you think may be in the loop when it comes to hearing about start-ups and ideas in search of investors. Then systematically get in touch with each person on your list. Let him or her know that you are looking for an investment opportunity in the form of an innovative business enterprise. Chances are you won't have to wait long before your phone rings.

Talk to Your Lawyer, Accountant, Banker

Typically and of necessity, lawyers and accountants and bankers are pretty well plugged into what's going on in a community or region. They tend to have a finger on the pulse of the marketplace because that's how they get customers and stay on top of business. Any and all of them are likely to know who is starting up a new venture, the details of the business, etc. In fact, their very own clients may be involved in new ventures and may be looking for investors, so your lawyer or accountant or banker can provide you a personal referral.

But don't leave it to chance. It's important to contact these professionals—and others you know who may be deeply involved in the business life of the community—to let them know that you are on the lookout for an innovative enterprise in which to invest. By reaching out this way, you will likely get to people who normally would be outside of your traditional circle.

Read the Local Paper

It sounds obvious, but it's worth restating that the local newspaper—and especially the business section—is one of the best places to search for new ventures and emerging invest-ment opportunities. Local papers can tell you who's doing what and where.

Surf the Internet

There are organizations that specifically sponsor investment in venture capital and other types of private equity ventures, and you can easily search for these on the Internet. A good place to start is www.privateequity.com. You might also search particu-lar industries or businesses you believe may be ripe for oppor-tunity. Be proactive, even aggressive, in contacting people you "meet" through the Web. You never know where such cyber-contacts can lead.

Always remember that when weighing an investment in someone else's idea, it is of paramount importance to do a thorough round of due diligence as part of the search. Read the business plan, have your lawyer review any contracts and documentation, and if there is neither a business plan nor documentation, think twice about investing in this person's venture.

But what if your aim is to create your own entrepreneurial venture? How do you approach it? Again, you have to search out the opportunities. Following are three ideas for where and how to start the thought process.

On-the-Job Opportunities

Begin with your own job. Is there a particular tool, service, or procedure that would make it easier to do, that would help you do your job faster or better or more cost-effectively? If you're a doctor, do you sense a need for a different way to organize patient information? Maybe you're a business owner frustrated by the inconsistencies in supplies delivery and certain there's a better way to do it—and perhaps you even know how. Or maybe you're a manager who has found a way your firm can improve customer service—and your revenue stream—but nobody in the corporation seems interested. Filling that gap profitably, improving on an existing product or process, may very well be your opportunity.

Look at the organization as a whole. Is there a quality service or product in your line that is limited in distribution, available to only a niche market or specific types of individuals? If so, do you see a way to get rid of the limits and increase the distribution of the service or product? Self-limiting distribution is a common business failing; widening the distribution for an existing service or product is typically a highly effective way to innovate a new business venture.

How about your industry? Where do you see it going in the future? Are there new avenues for potential growth? Taking the lead down such a path can be an exciting way to innovate an enterprise.

Your job gives you a front-row seat for addressing these questions and exploring these avenues. The answers may provide just the right idea for a business venture you're perfectly suited to undertake.

Opportunities in the Community

What's missing in your community? Are there enough laundromats? Movie theaters? Restaurants? Italian restaurants? Good Italian restaurants?

Perhaps a major company is located in your town; are there services you can provide that the company could use? For example, how about a limo service to take executives and clients to and from the nearest airport? Maybe, like Tom Kramer back in Chapter 1, you can be the outsourcer who gets the company's snowplowing contract. Alternatively, you could offer to counter the effects of winter and raise employee morale by providing fresh flowers, indoor plants, and outdoor landscaping for the company campus. What about a cleaning service? Catering service? Leasing fitness equipment for the company gym?

Filling a local need or a local business need can be an effective path to a successful innovative enterprise.

Letting Your Imagination Take Flight

Remember all the times in your life when you found yourself thinking up a putative product you were sure would "sell like hotcakes," or devising a service that could "make millions," or coming up with a solution to a problem or dilemma that seemed so simple it startled you? Now is the time to turn those what-if scenarios into business possibilities.

Want an example? Anyone reading this book is either a baby boomer or related to a baby boomer. So what's the next big, big thing for this aging generation—something they may be reluctant to accept? Or, what about something focused on supporting two-income households? How about a new product for the environmentally sensitive—like yourself—to enhance the environmental "friendliness" of the kitchen or bathroom?

Maybe there's an online service you keep telling yourself you need. If you need it, others no doubt need it too. Build it. Talk to your children: What's going on in their lives in school or high school or college? What about people in their thirties and forties: What are their needs and interests—and do those needs and interests bring any ideas to mind?

Let your imagination soar. There are many concepts that can translate into a practical idea. And great businesses often grow from practical ideas.

Step 2. Do the Due Diligence.

You now have one or more ideas about a potential business enterprise. Now comes the work of deciding whether any of it makes sense—whether the opportunity is real or not.

First, formalize the idea or ideas by writing a comprehensive description that includes the following points:

- The business need you have uncovered

- The product or service solution that will meet the need

- The organization or company that will produce and deliver the solution

Then name the idea: Executive Limos, Campus Landscaping, Midnight Cleaning. List your ideas by name and analyze the potential strengths of each and the challenges each is likely to confront. For example, it seems pretty obvious to you that Campus Landscaping would have a ready market in your area since there are two local midsized corporate campuses *plus* a corporate office park now under development on the other side of the interstate. The challenges include, however, the start-up costs for the equipment, whether leased or purchased, as well as securing the landscaping contract.

Executive Limos, in contrast, offers a nimble and inexpensive start-up. The key challenge with this business is determining whether there are a sufficient number of prospective clients to keep the business going—and growing—on a year-round basis.

Midnight Cleaning, on the other hand, probably has great growth potential—that is, once the office park is fully rented. The challenge will be to build in the flexibility to manage its operating costs by using temporary personnel.

The next step is to fill out a worksheet for your business ideas. Use the sample worksheet on page 154 as a guide to the blank template.

Once you've filled out the worksheet, identify the one business idea that combines the greatest strengths with the fewest challenges. When you've identified a business enterprise you would like to create from scratch, it's time to write a business plan.

Step 3. Do a Business Plan.

Business plan. It's one of those terms that is used often but seldom examined. Simply put, a business plan is a blueprint for the business you intend to start and operate and an outline of the actions you will take to operate it. Develop it from that perspective—as if it were going to be an operating "bible" you can refer to readily and easily.

Sample Worksheet

ENTERPRISE IDEA	STRENGTHS	CHALLENGES
Campus Landscaping	Ready market, growth potential	Costly start-up
Executive Limos	Clearly defined need, easy start-up	Personnel
Midnight Cleaning	Growth potential	Personnel

Your Worksheet Template

ENTERPRISE IDEA	STRENGTHS	CHALLENGES

At a minimum, your business plan should define the business need or opportunity, the nature of the business to create and to fill that need, the product or service, the market, your goals and objectives, your strategy and planned tactics, the business policies, and the financial realities of the business.

Begin by demonstrating the existence of the business need or opportunity you perceive; everything else will flow from this. The best way to demonstrate need or opportunity is through hard data: Who has the need or would respond to the product or service you're proposing? Why? How many individuals and/or companies are likely to respond? How will you reach them? Will they really be willing to pay for the product or service? How much?

Start researching the answers to these questions on the Internet and in your local library. Alternatively, you may find it worthwhile to invest in some primary research with actual potential customers. You can buy targeted e-mail lists from a range of providers—search the Internet and/or your local yellow pages—and you can then create or pay for the design of an appropriate survey to send out to the lists so you can answer the key business plan questions.

Research companies can also handle the entire process for you, designing the survey, targeting the audience, and conducting an online and/or telephone survey. This is typically a more costly proposition; depending on the length of the survey itself and the specificity required, the price could range from $5,000 to $100,000.

Once you've dimensioned the need or opportunity, however, you can go on to design your business proposition and figure out the cost of what you are trying to create. At a minimum you will need to research potential development costs, salaries, real estate, legal costs, and the like.

A business plan need not be lengthy. As you set about writing it, keep in mind your intended readers: people who might be persuaded to invest in your enterprise. In addition to wanting to know all the facts you can provide, they would probably like to see a three- to five-year outlook for the business and a list of the factors/events that will be required to make the business profitable. They will also be concerned about the range of risks the business is likely to encounter.

Here's what the table of contents of a typical business plan might include:

- Executive summary

- Description of the business

Need/opportunity

Solution

- Market analysis

- Management

- Operating strategies

- Financial projections

- Business risks

We've prepared a sample business plan you can use as a template; it's available on our Web site at www.millionairecorner .com. Your local library is likely to have several books on preparing a business plan as well. Make use of the full range of resources available.

Step 4. Double-Check Everything—With Professional Help.

Since you are about to go ask people for money—unless you are able to fund the entire enterprise yourself—it's a good idea to meet with your lawyer and accountant for a reassurance checkup. Your lawyer can assure you that you have the appropriate legal structure for your enterprise or can help you make the necessary adjustments. An accountant can add reassurance about the tax structure, if needed. These determinations will of course depend both on your personal situation as well as on the type of business you are creating.

Step 5. Approach Potential Investors.

The aim here is to produce a list of people and organizations you feel comfortable approaching and that might reasonably be capable of providing some funding if they can be persuaded to do so.

Start with family and friends. Who among them do you feel comfortable asking for money to fund your enterprise?

Then think about appropriate companies to approach—companies that could conceivably benefit from the business you are proposing and that might therefore consider staking the business to some extent.

Finally, don't forget about venture capital groups and private investors. Search the Internet for access to such investors. Again, our Web site, www.millionairecorner.com, makes available information about companies that invest in innovative enterprises.

With financial resources and a rock-solid plan, you have the basic necessities for starting up your innovative venture. So start hiring, start producing, start marketing, and open your doors. Good luck!

And don't forget: As soon as you've pulled in enough revenue, think hard about buying the building. . . .

A PORTRAIT OF PERPETUAL WEALTH: "MORE GOOD DECISIONS THAN BAD"

He grew up in cold, snowy Chicago, but today you will usually find Philip Chartoff under the warm Florida sun—maybe relaxing on the patio of his elegant, many-roomed "bungalow" or perhaps lunching, as is his habit, in the dining room of a nearby luxury beach resort. On the patio, he may wear an open collar, but in the resort dining room or any other public place, Chartoff is sure to be dressed in a jacket and tie.

The formality of his dress is the remnant of his up-bringing as the son of a Russian immigrant and in keeping with the style of the World War II generation Philip Chartoff represents. Back in Chicago, Chartoff's immigrant father had established a "hardware" business that sold industrial supplies. The business did well, and young Philip was able to attend a prestigious private school. When he was just a teenager, however, his father died. Philip soon found himself helping his mother run the business, and he might have stayed with it had World War II not intervened.

"I never considered myself smart," Chartoff says, but when the Army brass tested his IQ, "I was assigned to the unit responsible for counterintelligence." While he served, his mother continued to build up the hard-ware business with great success—not surprising in a wartime economy—and Philip came home to find him-self head of a dynamic and growing company.

He married into another successful entrepreneurial family. Laura Chartoff was the daughter of a continu-ally innovative entrepreneur who had personally invented a range of lighting systems; her family business was run by her brothers, but it was the original inventiveness that struck Philip Chartoff, who saw it at once as the key to growing a business and constantly refreshing its income stream.

Meanwhile, he was building his own family hardware business, establishing a strong wholesale network throughout the Midwest. He began to widen his product line, even selling radios, which Chartoff believed had great potential. In the 1960s, veteran investors were dismissing FM radio out of hand, but Philip Chartoff thought he saw promise in the idea, and he put his money where his mouth was, investing in the manufacturing process and buying a number of FM radio stations.

He also invested in other types of communication—including TV and magazines—and began to buy apartment buildings as well. It was these ventures—innovation and real estate—that really made his very considerable fortune.

In the late 1980s, Chartoff began to sell off many of his interests, and he and Laura retired to Florida. He did not retire from work, however. Now in his nineties and working out of an office he still visits on most days, Chartoff is actively involved in managing his investments—with the help of a full-time staff attorney and several additional professionals.

Most of the top investment banking firms in the United States and Europe—Goldman Sachs, Morgan Stanley, UBS, Northern Trust, and the like—have repeatedly approached Chartoff in an attempt to win the majority of his financial business, but he is reluctant to allow any one firm too much influence over his invest-ments. Rather than give all his business to one firm, he constantly shops for the best deal and people he can trust.

Most of his assets are in multiple trusts set up for various purposes. Investments range from private place-ment bonds to venture capital to the broad market, and Chartoff's investment philosophy remains relatively conservative. Chartoff demonstrated his forward vision in the innovative businesses he created, not to mention his real estate/apartment investments, which will con-tinue to provide steady income for him and his various grandchildren and beyond.

Still, Chartoff wants the grandchildren to value the need for thinking, planning, investing, and work-ing; he does not want them simply living off a trust fund. In fact, he has structured his trusts in such a way that provides incentives for that thinking, planning, in-vesting, and working—while discouraging sloth and indifference.

Where the capital markets are concerned, Chartoff takes the long view. "Some years a monkey can do bet-ter in the market than an investment manager," he says. "It's all a game of luck and thinking." His real interest remains in the innovations he helped fund and in the income-producing real estate he purchased—both a matter, he says, of "making more good decisions than bad decisions."

YOUR PERSONAL PLAN TO GET RICH, STAY RICH, AND PASS IT ON

SUMMARY CHECKLIST

Fill in the number or word answer, or check off the item you've completed.

Real Estate:

Total for down payment

Purchase price range

Loan amount

Property type

Caution questions

Cash flow analysis

Continually Innovative Enterprise:

Opportunity

Due diligence

Business plan

Professional advice

Investors

CHAPTER 8

THE WEALTHY USE ADVISORS

Once upon a time, there were brokers. They dressed in three-piece suits—they were all men, of course—and worked in wood-paneled offices on Wall Street, where most other New Yorkers rarely ventured, or in similar venues in Chicago, Detroit, Dallas, Los Angeles, San Francisco, and other cities around the nation. Back in the day these brokers emerged daily from their spacious offices for two-hour three-martini lunches. Rich people relied on these brokers to do what brokers do: buy and sell stocks to make the rich people even richer. In return, clients spoke about "my broker" in much the same way they might speak about their doctor or priest—as a trusted advisor into whose expert hands they willingly placed their lives and fortunes.

Those days are long gone.

The brokers are still here, to be sure. And some of them, women as well as men, still dress in suits. The wood-paneled offices have given way to high-tech consoles that plug the bro-kers into markets all over the world. And while the Wall Street area has become a hotbed of trendy restaurants and high-rises populated by young professionals, the two-hour lunches have given way to the half-hour gym workout. When brokers talk to-day, they talk directly to their clients—via phone or e-mail or face to face.

Today's brokers are go-getters. They have to be. They can no longer rest on the fact that they have a seat on the Exchange, and they can no longer simply match buyers with sellers of securities. They have to add value to each transaction because today they are competing with a range of other professionals—experts in an array of disciplines—for the advisor dollars of not just millionaires and mega-millionaires, but the mass affluent and less affluent as well. In fact, our research shows conclu-sively that just over half the households with assets of at least $100,000 reach out to some sort of advisor at some time for some purpose. And as the level of wealth rises, so does the use of advisors.

That constitutes perhaps the principal reason that financial advising today is such a different business from what it was even a decade or two ago. Simply put, there is a whole new population of people out there with the means and motivation to use financial advice today, and they are nothing at all like the exclusive band of wealthy clients who once spoke in hushed tones about "my broker."

Today's buyers of financial advice know a great deal more about finance and investments than their parents and grand-parents did. They live in a world where widespread access to all sorts of financial information is the norm. They see and hear 24-hour financial news, can listen to pundits ranting about stock picks and investment trends, can hear how the

Dow, the FTSE, the Dax, the Bourse, and the Hang Seng are doing almost minute by minute. Where investments are concerned, they already know the routine answers, the standard solutions, the off-the-shelf products.

Moreover, they are accustomed to being take-charge customers in just about every realm of their lives, and they have been empowered by technology to take charge of their finances personally. Many of these people shop and pay bills over the Internet, check their bank statements on their Black-Berrys, and find it easy and convenient to trade stocks online without bothering to go through a broker. They have a very real sense of responsibility for their own financial destiny—and for taking charge of that destiny. We know that's how you see it; that's precisely why you're reading this book. To you and countless others like you, the old attitude of "We know better; let us handle it for you" is simply a vestige of a time long since past.

The data on this is conclusive: A quarter of the wealthy—a full 25 percent—consider themselves completely "self-directed" in their financial decision-making. They do not use advisors under any circumstances. They do their own research, and conduct their own trading—typically on-line and often through a discount brokerage firm.

USING ADVISORS RELUCTANTLY

Ted Baird is a longtime techie who retired with a healthy fortune, a home in Beverly Hills, a good backhand in his tennis game, and the intention of managing his own finances.

Why not? He's been doing it as a sideline—and doing it pretty well—since back in the 1960s. At first Ted had dabbled in all sorts of investments, including options—a complex investment vehicle most stock market investors never get involved with. At one point, that left him the owner of several silos of corn in Iowa—not the result he was looking for. Still, it was a learning experience.

Ted was also an early investor in mutual funds when they first appeared on the scene, and he always "did okay" with his stock portfolio. In 1998 he became involved with a charting service so he could obtain all sorts of technical analysis on past market and investment trends; he also joined an investment club. He was justifiably pleased with his results and it confirmed his belief in his own expertise.

But the bear market that followed September 11, 2001, threw Ted for a loop. It was all too stressful, and for the first time in his life, he turned to a broker. The experience reminded him of why he did not want to deal with advisors. The broker, says Ted, "was in the market to buy and hold. I'm interested in three- to six-month trading. At my age, I'm not in for the long term. There may not be a long term!"

So Ted went back to his self-directed investing—for the most part. The truth is, there was just too much to do. He had taken on managing money for his wife and his brothers, and he had begun to become involved with estate planning. He was now dabbling, with some success, in limited partnerships, real estate, and other investments.

So Ted split the difference. His current strategy is to manage a portion of his assets on his own and to let a professional money manager take care of the rest. He wants to continue to be in charge of his own finances—"People have to learn about the markets and not trust blindly in advisors," he says—but he also wants to spend more time in his vacation home at Lake Tahoe. Reaching out to professionals lets him do both.

Our research makes it absolutely clear that three-fourths of the wealthy—and especially the wealthiest among them—still do reach out for professional financial advice. The reason? In their growing sophistication about finance and investing, they understand that the complexities of today's markets and the variety of options available make it necessary in some cases, and extremely helpful in others, to bring various kinds of expertise to bear on their deliberations and decision making.

The wealthy thus use these professional advisors for a variety of reasons—and in a variety of ways. And while the trend is clearly toward a collaborative relationship between client and advisor—a partnership of equals, so to speak—it is clear that advisors can certainly add value to the process of getting rich, staying rich, and passing it on.

That value can be particularly evident—and significant—as you begin to match your current asset allocation model to the benchmark model of perpetual wealth. Even the standard or "traditional" parts of the model—investment vehicles like stocks, bonds, insurance, and annuities, not to mention the more esoteric investments like derivatives and hedge funds— are now so varied and complex as to boggle the mind. At the very least, a guide through the thicket of investment options would be useful—an expert or experts who can help you understand the full range of your options and how each might best meet your needs.

Advisors can also add value as you begin to target perpetual wealth—especially if you are a novice at either investing in real estate or engaging in a continually innovative enterprise, or both. It's clear that both initiatives require substantive change in your personal balance sheet, and before you undertake such a change—as well as during the process—you may indeed find it beneficial to rely on the counsel of experts.

The trick is to use the right advisor for the right task, and to arrive prepared to extract the added value an advisor can offer. In this chapter, we'll look at the different kinds of advisors who may prove useful, and we'll show how everyone, from the mass affluent to mega-millionaires, can get the most out of their relationship with those advisors.

WHO IS AN ADVISOR?

It's a valid question. Anyone can hang up a shingle inscribed "Financial Advisor" and start doling out advice to those willing to pay for it. You can claim that your BA in accounting or your experience as a bond salesman or the crystal ball you have in the back room is all you need to make money for people, and if there are people willing to buy your advice, it is all perfectly legal.

It can also lead to confusion at the very least and charlatanism at the very worst, which is why a number of entities have come into being to provide credentials to those who meet their particular qualifications. A partial list of such credentials includes Accredited Estate Planner, Chartered Financial Analyst, Personal Financial Specialist, Registered Financial Consultant, and so on. The accreditation, chartering, specialization, or registering of such designations tells you that the practitioner has probably at least passed a course or two in the subject.

Where financial planning and advising are concerned, the picture is made clearer by the Certified Financial Planner Board of Standards, or CFP, which came into being back in 1985 to establish and enforce "uniform standards of competence, practice and ethics"* in financial planning and advising practices, which it certifies.

If and when you see the CFP mark, you know you're dealing with a Certified Financial Planner who has passed a licensing process similar to that required of Certified Public Accounts (CPAs). The CFP also recognizes, without endorsing, an array of other certifications, including those named in the foregoing paragraph, so a good place to check up on the certification claim of an advisor recommended by your brother-in-law or by the guy down the hall in your office is the CFP Web site, www.cfp.net.

What our research makes abundantly clear is that formally

---

* Certified Financial Planner Board of Standards Inc. Mission and History, http://www.cfp.net/aboutus/mission.

designated financial planners are only one category of advisors the rich use when seeking financial advice. In fact, we've defined eight types of advisors used by the wealthy in thinking about their finances and planning their investments:

- Full-service brokers

- Independent financial planners

- Investment managers

- Independent investment advisors

- Accountants

- Private bankers

- Trust officers

- Insurance agents

Although the terms are often used interchangeably, sometimes even by the advisors themselves—except for lawyers, of course—there are differences among the skills each can bring to the table. The differences, in fact, explain why these are the advisors of choice.

Full-service brokers, as has traditionally been the case, are licensed by the National Association of Securities Dealers (NASD) to trade stocks and mutual funds for clients. They may work for some of the huge well-known brokerage houses (sometimes called "wire houses") like Merrill Lynch, UBS, or Morgan Stanley; for midsize firms like Edward Jones or Raymond James; or for regional firms like Robert W. Baird or Janney Montgomery Scott. Brokers may also present themselves as financial advisors, a term that may vary in meaning from broker to broker. The caveat with brokers is that they are paid a commission on the stock or fund they sell (as well as other fees), so a broker who acts as a financial advisor stands to generate more revenue on the particular stocks and funds they sell for their firms.

Independent financial planners, especially those certified by the CFP board and qualified to display the board's mark—CFP—are planning specialists trained to take a holistic view of your entire financial picture. They will consider estate planning issues, tax planning, and long-term investment planning. Financial planners typically charge on a fee-only basis.

Investment managers manage a portfolio and typically specialize in specific types of securities or asset classes. Thus you may have a bond investment manager or a short-term equity investment manager, or the like. Mostly, the investment managers we have in mind tend to be in midsized to small companies that also provide asset management services to individuals, to retirement funds, or to endowment and foundation funds. These advisors usually charge asset-based fees.

Independent investment advisors provide advice on investments and typically use the products and services from a range of financial firms. An investment advisor will not actively manage a fund portfolio but will rather manage a client's portfolio invested in multiple funds. Larger clients—institutions, for example—may appoint a number of investment managers to manage their particular pool of money. Investment advisors may work either on commission or for an asset-based fee on whatever portion of your portfolio they manage. Sometimes, although it is rare, investment advisors charge a flat fee.

Together, the skills of investment managers and independent investment advisors often come together in the designation "wealth manager." Although an organization known as the

American Academy of Financial Management does charter a practitioner known as a Chartered Wealth Manager, the term remains nebulous enough in general usage that anyone can claim it. Typically, however, a wealth manager would serve as an overall financial quarterback for the wealthy—someone capable of planning, advising, and executing a comprehensive financial life plan.

Accountants are of course the bedrock of financial planning and advising, for they provide the measurements of your financial situation that should be the basis of any resource allocation or investment decision. They also understand and bring to bear the tax implications of any investment, financial instrument, or transaction.

Many investment banks devote resources to a private banking division, catering to high-net-worth clients only. For these clients, **private bankers** provide a range of services—typically, whatever is asked of them—from investment advice to estate planning, from structuring a pension to advice on charitable giving. Private bankers often establish a relationship with a client through a credit need, so business owners tend to be approached and solicited by private bankers.

Trust officers are the bank's experts on estate planning; a trust officer will typically be a member of a wealthy client's private banking team.

So how do the wealthy use each of these different kinds of advisors, and what does the usage pattern tell us? Our research answers the question.

WHICH ADVISORS ARE USED

Perhaps the most profound finding of our research remains that fundamental statistic showing that nearly three-quarters of the wealthy use a primary professional advisor. It's true no matter how rich they are, and it's true no matter how old they are. In fact, the percentage of those using an advisor is remarkably uniform across all wealth segments. And while all age groups clearly reach out for professional advice in great numbers, older individuals are slightly more likely than younger wealthy people to do so.

That age distinction may account to some extent for the corollary finding that the type of advisor most commonly used is the full-service broker. Since "my broker" was just about the only game in town back in the 1960s and 1970s, he or she still gets the lion's share of client dependence and dollars. True, brokers lost a big share of the market in the wake of September 11, 2001, and they have yet to regain that overwhelming dominance. But they remain the advisor of choice across all wealth segments.

Among the other advisor choices, the picture is less clear, with the choice differing across wealth segment and by age.

THE OLDER THEY GET,
THE LESS SMART THEY THINK THEY ARE

Although the mass affluent, millionaires, and mega-millionaires all continue to seek advice from professional advisors, older individuals are more likely than younger ones to use an advisor.

The reasons seem to be both generational and situational. Older individuals who built their wealth during the 1960s and 1970s had little choice among financial advisors. In fact, they had two basic choices: their broker or themselves. Today's upcoming wealthy, however, have long confronted a range of advising options—as well as an almost dizzying array of investment product possibilities. They are thus less inclined to take the "default position" of relying on a single advisor like a broker. Moreover, many of these younger wealthy individuals have also grown up in the era of discount and online brokerage, and they simply enjoy investing for themselves, often in the comfort of their own homes, without paying a hefty fee to do so.

It will be interesting to see if these younger wealthy individuals turn more to professional advisors as they get older.

WHAT ADVISORS ARE USED FOR

Most of the mega-millionaire households who use professional advisors use them for specialized needs or for a special "event." They may be contemplating a change of career or a life change of some sort—change of residence, marriage, divorce, retirement. They may be considering investing in a new enterprise or starting their own entrepreneurial venture.

Only a small percentage of mega-millionaires—14 percent at the time of this writing—consider themselves advisor dependent, or rely on a professional to make most or all of their financial or investment decisions.

Interestingly, while about a quarter of wealthy households

use no professional advisor at all, a similar average percentage say they pick the brains of professional advisors, listen to their recommendations, but make the decision themselves. The former might be termed completely self-directed: they feel no need for professional advice, and they enjoy managing their own money. The latter might be termed advisor-assisted; 23 percent of mega-millionaires describe themselves as such. In their case, reaching out to a professional advisor is just one of several steps they take as part of their decision-making process. They typically look to numerous different sources of information, so the professional financial advisor's advice may rank as just one element among a number of equal elements that bear on the final decision.

Mega-Millionaire Advisor Dependency

Special Event You make most of your own investment decisions but use an investment professional or advisor for specialized needs only		Advisor-Dependent You rely upon an investment professional or advisor to make most or all of your investment decisions

25%	38%	23%	14%

Self-Directed You make all of your own investment decisions without the assistance of an advisor	Advisor-Assisted You regularly consult with an investment professional or advisor and may get additional information yourself, but you make most of the final decisions

In fact, what we call the selective use of professional advisors is increasingly the norm. By this we mean not only that investors call on professional advisors only as needed, but that they also want to work with their advisors in a collaborative way. That can make a substantive difference to the advisors themselves, for they find that collaborating with clients on a partnership basis often requires more time, more expertise, and more resources than it does when clients let advisors choose every investment option and make every financial decision. As we said at the beginning of this chapter, those days are very definitely on the way out.

Another aspect of this trend toward selective collaboration is the practice of many (38 percent) investors of using an advisor to consult on only some assets or some part of the portfolio. Of those who "withhold" assets from an advisor's view and influence, the overwhelming majority say it is simply because they enjoy investing those particular assets themselves. They like making investment decisions on their own—at least, in these particular circumstances or for these particular assets. Many say they don't want all their eggs in one basket in any way, shape, or form—including in the hands of a single advisor. Others say the assets they withhold from an advisor are for speculative investments—high-risk investments that an advisor would probably advise against in the first place. Some say they like to see how well their investments do versus the results their advisor achieves. In fact, the more advisor-dependent an investor is in general, the greater the desire to invest some assets separately as a comparison test of the advisor's performance.

Enjoyment, not testing, is actually the reason given by those wealthy households that use no advisors at all. Nearly 40 percent of such households claim they enjoy managing their own money and simply don't feel they need any help doing it. Only a few—17 percent—think they are smarter or more knowledgeable than a professional advisor; it's really that investing has become a form of recreation to these people, perhaps like an interactive game. Actually, in the case of more than a quarter of those avoiding advisors, the cost of professional advice is the issue; they simply don't want to pay for information they're pretty sure is readily available and for advice they're pretty sure they don't need.

WHICH ADVISOR SHOULD THEY USE?

Hone your advisor selection savvy as you determine which kind of professional expertise is most appropriate for each of the scenarios that follow. All of the people looking for advisors qualify—at the least—as members of the mass affluent. They're all bright, successful, and pretty sophisticated, and all believe they need expert professional advice. Choose from among the following financial advisors for them; they may require more than one.

- Full-service broker

- Independent financial planner

- Investment manager

- Independent investment advisor

- Accountant

- Private banker

- Trust officer

Scenario 1.

Beth is fifty-seven years old, divorced, and securely employed as a high-level state worker with excellent health benefits and a good pension. After her divorce, she managed to "buy out" her ex-husband, so she now has free and clear title to the house in which she hopes to live for the rest of her life. She expects to retire in ten years at the mandatory retirement age for her state agency, and she wonders what she can do between now and then to assure that she will have as much retirement income as she possibly can.

Beth should see a   .

Scenario 2.

Martin and Melanie are not just husband and wife but also are co-owners of a small but successful family business. To keep the business successful, they've decided they need to upgrade and update some equipment and processes, and they are willing to invest some key assets as well as extend their line of credit to do so. At the same time, they have realized that they need estate planning advice. After all, they're approaching their fifties and are childless, although they are close to Melanie's niece and excited about the recent birth of a grandnephew. But the fact is that they really haven't thought much past the next step in the life of the business, and it's time they should.

Martin and Melanie should see a   .

Scenario 3.

David is a financially savvy, highly motivated investor who has long enjoyed managing his own assets. Lately, however, he has found the job of doing so time-consuming, tedious, and downright bothersome—and it has begun to show in the performance of his investments. David realizes it's time he share the job of managing his own wealth with a real asset management expert. He knows he is not interested in mutual funds but wants to pool his assets into fixed-income investments and is looking for the best-in-class to take on the task.

David should see a   .

Scenario 4.

Mary is thirty-nine years old and a very successful investment banker. She has finally decided that she will probably not marry—she feels she is not cut out for marriage—and she has been reading lots of articles about single women buying their own homes and other articles about single women having babies on their own. She is inclined to do both. But as much as she knows about investments and about realizing superior returns on investments, Mary is confused about how such changes in her life might affect her wealth—and about how her wealth can make the changes in her life happen.

Mary should see a   .

ANSWERS

Scenario 1.

Ideally, Beth should see a financial planner. But if cost is a factor, or if she wants a simple and straightforward investment plan, her best bet is probably to go to a full-service broker and invest in a diverse portfolio of growth stocks.

Scenario 2.

Martin and Melanie should see their private banking team. They need a trust officer to work with them as they develop their estate plan and create a trust to ensure their assets are bequeathed appropriately and are appropriately managed after their deaths. The trust officer should refer them to a law firm that is a preferred partner of the bank for drafting the trust agreements and wills. The private banker will also work closely with Martin's and Melanie's accountant who can tie together whatever steps they take in terms of understanding the tax implications and riding herd on the transactions they execute.

Scenario 3.

David's best bet is to see an independent investment advisor who can discern his needs and goals and then refer him to the right investment managers specializing in the solutions that meet those needs and can reach David's goals.

Scenario 4.

Mary's first stop should be the office of a lawyer who is an expert in estate planning. At the moment, she has no designated heir, but as she is clearly interested in having a child, that will change. Once her newfound attorney has structured an estate plan that makes sense, Mary's next visit should be to a financial planner who can lay out her more immediate financial needs and solutions.

> Finally, she will need an investment manager who can structure and monitor the right portfolio to accommodate the changes she is now seeking in her life—and to ensure the long-term viability of her overall estate plan.

ADVISOR ALLEGIANCE

For whatever purpose the wealthy use advisors in this increasingly selective, collaborative investor-advisor environment, one thing is certain: Once the wealthy individual or household chooses the advisor, he/it tends to remain a loyal client. Almost half of wealthy people using an advisor in some capacity have been doing so with that same advisor for more than ten years. In fact, the very wealthiest among us insist they would transfer their assets should their advisor move to a new firm. In short, the relationship between a wealthy investor and his or her primary professional advisor is very personal.

What's more, our research confirms that those now using an advisor expect to be using the same advisor in the same capacity for the foreseeable future. Even those who make the least use of advisors say they have little intention of dropping or replacing their primary professional advisor. In fact, those who use advisors the least are the most likely to add another financial advisor—all part of seeking information and advice from multiple sources before they make the decision on their own.

What's at the heart of this kind of loyalty? "Heart" may be the answer. Foremost among the reasons given for allegiance to an advisor is the investor's subjective sense that "my advisor understands my appetite for risk." In addition, investors who use advisors believe the advisor serves their interests over the interests of the advisor's firm. They also appreciate the advisor's expertise and the resources on which he or she can draw in serving the investor's needs.

Pressed to analyze the drivers of their loyalty to advisors, the wealthy say that responsiveness to requests tops the list, with the advisor's knowledge and expertise a very close second. In fact, wealthy investors say that the thing that is most decisive in their loyalty is that their advisor provides a backup contact if he or she is not available—another person who can speak to the investor and return the investor's phone call quickly. Certainly, achieving the sought-after return on investments was of prime importance, but it was the advisor's responsiveness that made for loyalty and allegiance, not just the expected appreciation of assets.

Bottom line? What counts in this business relationship is the personal—a subjective sense of trust that the advisor is working for the client and knows how to do it well.

HOW YOU CAN MAKE THE BEST USE OF AN ADVISOR

Perhaps the first step toward getting the most out of your relationship with an advisor is to recognize (a) your limitations and/or (b) the special added value a primary professional advisor can provide. You use specialist experts in numerous other fields of your life—certainly in medicine, when your car needs repair, in setting up your home computer or entertainment center—so why wouldn't you reach out to an expert in this most important realm: your finances?

But be sure you know what kind of expertise you require. Just as you wouldn't go to a cardiologist to heal a broken bone, you don't want to head to a discount brokerage house when deciding whether or not to invest in your neighbor's new venture. Go through the list provided at the start of this chapter and determine what your needs really are. If you're not sure, you may want to turn to an accountant to take a look at your entire money situation, or to a financial planner to take an overall look at your financial options.

Once you know what you're looking for, it's time to choose among advisors. As our research confirms, the most common way to find a primary professional advisor is by a referral from a friend or family member. Nothing counts as much as a personal recommendation from someone you know—or someone known to someone you know—who has had a good experience with the advisor.

If you have no referral, you can find advisors at most brokerage firms, bank branches, mutual fund companies, even insurance and accounting and tax preparation offices. Or simply check newspaper ads and the yellow pages for the designation you're seeking.

Whether you are acting on a referral or pulling a name out of a hat, be sure to do the appropriate due diligence on the advisor and the firm with which he or she is affiliated. You are looking for performance results, of course, but also for stability and the kind of responsiveness that is so prized by the wealthiest American households.

Some advisors are "affiliated" with specific firms. An "affiliated" advisor works for a large well-known firm that sells some of its own products and services. This includes firms such as Merrill Lynch, Morgan Stanley, UBS, and similar names. About 68 percent of wealthy investors use "affiliated" advisors. When working with an "affiliated" advisor it's important to ascertain not only that products from all providers are available at the firm, but also that the firm's proprietary products are not "pushed" disproportionately—that is, to the exclusion of other products that might better serve a client's needs. That would mean the firm has given top priority to its own best interests, not the interests of its client, and that's a firm to stay away from.

Your particular interest in reviewing a firm's performance will be to see how the firm performs vis-à-vis people in similar circumstances to yours and with similar financial needs. If you have assets of $20 million and the firm has never dealt with a portfolio valued at more than $200,000, you're probably in the wrong place altogether.

The reverse is equally true: A firm catering to the $20-million investor is probably not going to bother much with a starter portfolio under $200,000. You want an expert advisor, but you want an advisor who will understand your needs and your goals first and foremost.

How will you find all this out? Ask—and if you don't get answers, move on. Any firm should be more than willing to disclose the answers to all the questions you have. At a minimum, those questions should include:

- How long has the firm been in business?

- What is the firm's five-year track record for return on investment? How does that compare to the industry benchmark?

- Are financial planning services offered, and are they offered by Certified Financial Planners—CFPs? Will the CFPs provide personal references?

- Are planning and advising services customized or standardized—or a combination of the two? What's the combination?

- Is a tax expert available?

- What is the ratio of proprietary products to unaffiliated products in an average portfolio?

Again, if answers to these and other questions are not readily forthcoming, there is probably something the firm does not want you to know. Look elsewhere.

MONITORING PERFORMANCE

You've signed up with an advisor you like and trust, you've been surveyed and queried, a financial plan has been drawn up for you, and you're taking most, if not all, of the advice your new primary professional advisor offers you. Now what?

Well, first of all, if you don't hear from your primary professional advisor in the next quarter, subtract points for his or her professionalism. If you don't hear in the quarter after that, strike the notion of "primary." If you go more than half a year without a personal communication from your advisor, strike the advisor.

We are not talking about your account statement—certainly the most important communication you will receive—or about newsletters, announcements of seminars, or interactive quizzes on the Web site. All of those are good things to have, and all are automatically generated by the firm. We are talking instead about hearing regularly from your advisor with good news as well as bad, with new ideas and general conversation simply to "catch up."

For one thing, such communication will tell you that your advisor is being proactive rather than reactive—an essential for successful performance. You want an advisor who is up-to-date on market shifts and world events and how they impact your financial life. Hearing from an advisor on such matters is evidence that he or she is on top of the situation.

Besides, while all our research makes it clear that wealthy investors today are changing the way they want to interact with their advisors and the expectations they have of those advisors, one thing hasn't changed: the need to feel there's a human being you can trust at the other end of the relationship. The best advisors build that trust by keeping your financial picture in mind, knowing your goals, understanding your risk tolerance, and working in your best interests—and they evidence that by keeping in touch. The advisor who does all that can add immeasurable value to your asset allocation portfolio and your ability to grow your wealth.

YOUR ACCOUNTANT AND YOUR LAWYER

It's a good idea to ask your accountant and your lawyer to take a look at any real estate or entrepreneurial business transaction you're seriously considering, as well as to review any plan by an advisor that calls for substantive investment or significant change. Business owners and professionals in particular should already be aware of the critical role these two experts play in their financial life. But anybody embarking on a plan to grow wealth should certainly have a lawyer and accountant who will understand the tax implications of any financial plan, can assess the legal structures that may be needed, and can advise you about the potential impact on your overall estate planning goals.

In fact, if you don't now have a relationship with a practicing attorney at a firm that has a robust estate planning department as well as proven expertise in stock options and restricted stocks, and with an accountant who can always provide an accurate measurement of your financial situation, now is the time to get one. Using the same methodology as you would to identify the right financial advisor, find the right lawyer and accountant, and develop professional relationships you can count on with both.

A PORTRAIT OF PERPETUAL WEALTH: ADVISOR-DEPENDENT—AND GLAD OF IT

Trish Dawson has a home now—on the beach in Mexico—and a full and happy life to go with it. But it wasn't always so.

It should have been. Trish grew up wealthy, the daughter of a Texas oil magnate. She lacked for nothing, and she had few demands. By all rights, she should have been able to live life pretty much as she wanted it—without burdening or hurting anyone, and without making waves. Of course, no life is trouble-free, and not every life turns out the way you expect, but Trish certainly came up against some unpleasant obstacles.

Fortunately, the money was there to cushion the blows somewhat, and Trish was lucky enough to be blessed with excellent financial advice. In her case, the advice was provided by a team of professionals, led by a trust officer, who advised her on her trust fund starting on her twenty-first birthday—the day it took effect—and who understood Trish, her goals, and her character. While Trish's life had its ups and downs, her trust fund remained a steady anchor—thanks to the advisors on whom she relied.

Her adulthood certainly didn't start out badly. Mostly, Trish was eager to marry, settle down, and raise a family, so when she met Mr. Right during her senior year of college, it seemed that all of her dreams were coming true. She eschewed all the advice about prenuptial agreements, certain, as young brides tend to be, that hers was a match made in heaven that could not possibly go wrong.

Trish and Howard settled in a suburb outside Dallas, and Howard took a job with one of the Dawson oil companies. But it didn't work out. Howard thought that as Husband of the Heiress, he should start at the top, while Trish's father clearly expected his son-in-law to work his way up. Says Trish of the two men in her life, "They never really got along. I shouldn't have let Howard take the job."

Howard eventually left the job—and the family business and the oil industry. But he had a hard time finding anything that suited him. He drifted from sales job to sales job, and Trish began to feel that she was supporting the marriage with her trust fund. Then one night, while Howard was away on one of his many sales trips, Trish called his room and a woman answered. That was the end of her marriage. "The hard part," she says, "was that I was forced to pay support to him for many years. In retrospect, I often wondered if it had always been about the money."

Trish spent the next few years traveling the world and learning new things. Suddenly passionate about art, she began to spend a lot of time in New York City. At a nightclub there, she met Paul, a real estate developer based in Florida. After a short romance, they married, and Trish moved to a lovely home just outside Sarasota. This time her family and her advisors made sure the appropriate prenuptial agreement was in place. Trish went along, but once again she felt this caution wasn't necessary. For one thing, she knew that this time her marriage would last forever. Besides, her new husband had what she believed to be substantial assets of his own.

But again it didn't work. Paul's substantial assets were highly leveraged in his real estate holdings. He began to pressure Trish to invest in some of his developments, but her primary professional advisor recommended against the idea and managed to keep Trish's assets separate from Paul's—and undiminished.

In addition to the money issue, Trish was bored. Having lived the life of an international traveler, she found suburban life in Florida dull by comparison. It was not surprising that rifts soon appeared in the marriage. Trish desperately wanted to have children, but Paul had adult children from a previous marriage and had no interest in a new family. As his real estate investments floundered, so did the marriage.

It was during the divorce process that Trish first discovered the beach in Mexico where she now makes her home. She has become part-owner of a gallery, has begun to paint on her own, and still travels—throughout Mexico as well as around the world—shopping for the art to display in her gallery. She is close to her nieces and nephews, who call and visit her often, and she has a wide circle of friends. "Living here has helped me to identify what is important," Trish says, "and that is sitting back and listening."

Finally, the financial security she has always had, well tended for her by valued advisors, has brought her the contentment she deserves. In return, Trish has invested herself and her money in the local community that welcomed her and made her feel, at long last, at home.

CHAPTER 9

THE MILLIONAIRES' CORNER

Up to now, we've concentrated on the what and how of getting rich, staying rich, and passing it on. We've done the explication and detailed the execution—revealing the two secrets to perpetual wealth, and how to tap them. It's all been evidence-based, as the current phrase has it, with every conclusion deriving inescapably from the hard research we've conducted over time.

The same can be said of the details we are about to present in this chapter, even though the chapter is about some highly subjective, very elusive qualities: attitudes, values, quality of lifestyle—all revealed in the way the rich think about their wealth and what they do with it.

These are perhaps the real secrets about getting and staying rich. The inside story isn't just about numbers, percentages, and the benchmark model. Most wealthy people had no idea they've been following a model. Besides, there's nothing particularly hush-hush about owning real estate and investing in a continually innovative enterprise. In fact, both are pretty public initiatives.

The real secrets of the perpetually wealthy are the why and wherefore of the process—what people seek to be rich *for* and what underpins the material prosperity they have achieved. As this chapter shows, the real X-factor from the millionaires' and mega-millionaires' corner is that these people lead very structured lives, work hard, and are neither reckless nor sparing. They seek their wealth for security against illness and disaster, to ensure themselves a high standard of living throughout their lives, to give well and to live well—and they use their wealth for just those purposes.

None of this is particularly surprising when we remember who these people are. They are primarily senior corporate executives, business owners and entrepreneurs, physicians and other professionals—managers, consultants, technical specialists, attorneys and the like. The very wealthiest among them are those who have created or who own a privately held business or professional practice that continues to refresh their wealth. In fact, as discussed earlier, the percentage of business owners increases as one moves up the wealth scale, as does the value of the business itself.

We compared in the chart below the values of two types of private business holdings—a professional practice (i.e. doctor's practice or law firm) versus a privately held business. As you can see, the wealthiest individuals, those with over $25 million, are the most likely to be business owners.

Mega-Millionaire Ownership of a Professional Practice or Privately Held Business

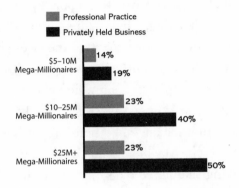

In other words, these people are no strangers to the world of work. They have valuable experience, have paid their dues, and have earned what they have. Today, in fact, two-thirds of all the perpetually wealthy are wealthy enough to be retired or semiretired, and most live on investment income rather than earned income. In fact, the richer the household, the greater the percentage of its income is derived from investments rather than work.

HARD WORK

But it is work, hard work, that is the true source of perpetual wealth—so say the perpetually wealthy. True, many credit education as a key factor in their material success, and certainly in the case of skilled professionals, that appears to be a sound and reasonable judgment. Many—82 percent—also credit native intelligence as a key factor in securing their wealth (e.g., smarter investing). And a great number of the wealthy— 65 percent, including the wealthiest among them—attribute their success to risk taking, while 62 percent attribute it to luck or chance. And a few acknowledge that they were born with silver spoons in their mouths through some form of inheritance.

Of these contributors to wealth, just about all of them are in the hands of the individual investor. While luck is not something you can summon at will, there are those who say we make our own luck. Maybe we do so learning how to invest smartly, by taking calculated risks, and by getting all the education we can get. Certainly, working hard is something in our own hands, and virtually all the wealthy across all wealth segments and age differences (97 percent) agree that it is hard work that got them rich in the first place, is keeping them rich, and is the reason they have wealth to pass on to their heirs.

How the Mega-Millionaires Say They Got Rich

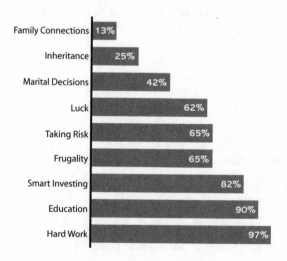

In fact, the hard work is typically on a 24/7 basis. There is a sense in which the work—at least the work of managing their wealth—occupies the wealthy on a full-time basis. Half work while vacationing, and half—perhaps the same half—put in more than 40 hours a week on their formal occupation. But it is the job of managing their wealth that seems to occupy the wealthy on any day at any time. If not wholly engaged every minute of the day in their work or in managing their wealth, the wealthy nevertheless see themselves as "on call"—that is, that they must be available on a moment's notice to attend to the matters related to the accumulation and maintenance of their wealth.

Average Hours Mega-Millionaires Work Per Week

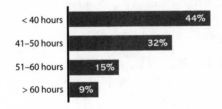

COMMITTED TO SAVING

Whatever their annual income, the rich are committed to saving and investing their money. This is a secret that is evidently being well kept from the rest of America, as the personal savings rate of most Americans has dipped into negative territory in recent years, sinking as low as −1.8 percent in 2005. In stunning contrast, the savings and investment rate of rich Americans averages a whopping 23 percent.

And indeed, the richer people are, the more they save and invest. While those in the $5 million to $10 million range save at a rate of 19 percent, the very richest, with net assets of more than $25 million, save and invest at a rate of 31 percent.

This commitment to saving and investing is instructive. While economists attribute much of the decline in American savings rates to the housing boom of the early part of the century, which made people "feel" wealthy enough to use their savings for big-ticket items, they also point out that an aging population is now using its savings to live in retirement.

Those who turned the two keys to getting rich, staying rich, and passing it on during their prime earning years have the wherewithal not just to enjoy a comfortable and secure retirement, but also to continue to save and invest during their retirement years. The savings secret of the wealthy may therefore serve as an object-lesson—especially to those in their prime who persist in using up every bit of their disposable income.

How much do you save? While the 23 percent savings rate of the rich may seem unreachable, you may actually be saving more than you think. Do you have a 401(k) plan at work? If not, take advantage of it as an automatic savings vehicle and have the money for the plan automatically deducted from your pretax paycheck. If you do, you'll realize savings of up to $15,000—$20,000 if you are fifty or older—per year. You can also arrange for an automatic savings plan at your bank; many people say it's far easier to save when they don't have to remember to set aside the money every week or month—just let the bank do it for you. If you never have access to the money in the first place—because it's being automatically deducted for your retirement or into a special-purpose savings account—it's much easier to save. "Paying yourself first," as this is often referred to, is a real key to mastering the habits of the perpetually wealthy.

Not surprisingly, the more your wealth grows, helped along by those automatic savings, the easier it is to save, and the more you can put aside for savings. This also assumes, of course, that you can keep your personal spending habits under control.

HEDGING AGAINST RETIREMENT
AND HEALTH CONCERNS

In fact, the retirement years of the perpetually wealthy are routinely funded by the investments they have made throughout their life. Social security and other pensions—typically from company-sponsored retirement plans—represent less than a quarter of the retirement funds on which the wealthy rely. Rather, they are living on their investments first and foremost, as well as on IRAs and annuities.

This reveals one of the key reasons the wealthy get wealthy in the first place. The rich offer no uniform "magic number" as to what they will need for retirement, just an abstract vision of "enough" to ensure that the retirement years are secure and comfortable.

In fact, it may be surprising that setting specific financial goals is not a particular habit of the wealthy. The younger wealthy, as well as those using advisors on a selective and collaborative basis, are more likely to be working toward specific dollar-figure objectives; but for the most part, the goal remains that abstract idea of comfort and security, and the wealthy find it only marginally relevant to attach a number to that goal.

Not surprisingly, the older wealthy feel certain that they now have enough to ensure that goal, while the younger foresee needing still more in their distant retirements; no matter what their present wealth, they are sure it will not be sufficient for the retirement they envision. But of course, the definition of sufficiency will vary from individual to individual, and it will depend on factors that often have little to do with money and everything to do with personality, insecurities, and expectations.

However much "enough" is, it must embrace concerns the wealthy have about their health, the health of their spouses, and certainly about the health of aging parents. The richer they are, the less the level of concern, perhaps because they know they will have at least the material wherewithal to deal with whatever occurs. But worries over the effects of aging and the costs of care giving in old age are clearly major reasons the rich sought to get rich in the first place.

So how do the rich define their financial goals? They're probably very similar to your own goals:

- 84 percent want to ensure they have a comfortable standard of living during retirement.

- 81 percent want to maintain their current standard of living.

- 71 percent want to minimize taxes.

- 64 percent want to build a sizable portfolio.

- 54 percent want to fund a child's or grandchild's education.

NEITHER EXTRAVAGANT NOR ASCETIC

One of the surprising secrets of those wealthy enough to pass wealth on is the moderate way in which they live. We all tend to think that if we had the kind of wealth the perpetually wealthy enjoy, we would lavish it on fancy cars, fabulous homes, incredible vacations, and such tokens of wealth as fine clothing and beautiful jewelry. But in fact, the lives of even mega-millionaires are routinely unostentatious.

Most spend less than $10,000 a year on clothing—per household. We know office receptionists and salaried truck drivers who outspend that. Almost a quarter of the perpetually wealthy don't buy jewelry at all. Very few are into Bugattis, Porsches, or gas-guzzling Hummers. Fewer still have run out and purchased yachts with their wealth. And only 2 percent of the wealthy actually own or lease a private plane.

What they do spend money on is just what they said they wanted money for—a comfortable standard of living. Household staff—including cleaning, lawn care, cooking or catering, and possibly the proverbial pool man—cost more than $10,000 annually for just over a quarter of the perpetually wealthy.

And where they do tend to spend lavishly is on vacation and recreation. The wealthy do not stint when they travel; they like to go first class, and they like to enjoy themselves without having to watch every dime. They also like belonging to country clubs, golf clubs, tennis clubs, and other similar organizations that give them unlimited and perhaps private access to the recreation and settings they enjoy.

A lot of the perpetually wealthy—just under half, in fact,—own their own vacation or "second" home. Some of them—11 percent—own a third home, or even more. For the most part, these additional homes afford recreational possibilities not available, or not as readily available, at the household's primary residence. Ski house, beach house, mountain hideaway, lakefront cottage: The choices are as varied as the recreational preferences of the families.

GIVING WELL, LIVING WELL

Among a preponderance of wealthy households, great importance is attached to charitable giving. Environmental causes, disaster relief, cultural institutions, and health-care initiatives all get a share of the philanthropic dollars the wealthy dole out, but the biggest recipients are religious organizations or churches. Especially in recent years, such organizations have received almost a third of the charitable contributions the wealthy give, although the wealthiest of the wealthy give less to these organizations than other wealth segments do.

The second largest group of recipients of charitable dollars from the wealthy are colleges and schools and such social service organizations as United Way, Red Cross, and others. Again, the stand-out difference among wealth segments is that the very wealthiest, those least likely to give to religious organizations, are most likely to give to colleges and schools.

That more than half of the wealthy cite charitable giving as an important part of their lives is informative. A number claim to take the giving yet further, spending some of their leisure time doing charitable volunteer work. The very favorite leisure activity of the perpetually wealthy, however, is travel. It is cited twice as often as the second favorite, reading.

To show they're no couch potatoes, whether traveling or not, the next three favorite pastimes of the perpetually wealthy are golf, exercise, and gardening—all of which require some physical effort. Then comes charitable volunteer work, followed by a range of disparate activities—sports, tennis, spending time with family, cultural pursuits, fishing, dining out, bridge, investing, working, and gambling. With respect to how they like to spend their time, therefore, the rich are not very different from you and me; they simply have the material wherewithal and the time to indulge their interests more readily than the rest of us.

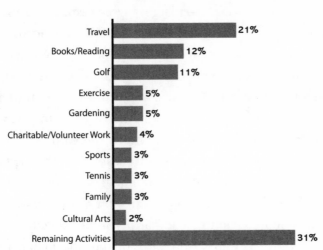

How the Rich Spend Their Leisure Time

Activity	Percentage
Travel	21%
Books/Reading	12%
Golf	11%
Exercise	5%
Gardening	5%
Charitable/Volunteer Work	4%
Sports	3%
Tennis	3%
Family	3%
Cultural Arts	2%
Remaining Activities	31%

Again, the very ordinariness of their leisure pursuits throws into sharper relief this basic secret of getting rich, staying rich, and passing it on: The goal is not to create a spectacle or live in an outsized way, but rather to ensure an overall standard of living that protects, assures comfort, and is secure for this lifetime and for the generations to come.

A PORTRAIT OF PERPETUAL WEALTH:
STILL A CHANCE TO DO IT RIGHT

Fashionable and energetic, Donna Anderson almost literally sparkles with intelligence and charm. A partner in one of the world's largest and most successful law firms, she is the embodiment of professional success, and she looks and acts the part with confidence and pizzazz.

She gained her success by working very hard, although it certainly did not hurt to have been born with an extremely good brain. Still, Donna earned everything that came her way: She was valedictorian of her high school class—a large, highly respected suburban high school in the Midwest—attended Dartmouth College, and then graduated from Harvard Law School.

Immediately upon graduation from Harvard, Donna joined a prestigious Chicago law firm that was thrilled to have her. She began working her way up to partner level—and got there quickly. Shortly thereafter, a group of her colleagues broke away en masse from the firm to join a not very dissimilar firm, equally prestigious and equally old-line. The opportunity for Donna was the chance to become the lead partner in her specific area of expertise, so after serious thought, she joined the breakaway group and went to the rival firm.

Unfortunately, it soon became clear that the firm to which the group had broken away was mired in serious problems. In fact, in only a few short years, this old and once respected firm went belly-up. It was an extremely stressful experience for Donna. Still a young woman, she became painfully aware of how the retirement funds and other benefits that constitute a law partner's long-term security could disappear—almost overnight.

Happily, Donna was quickly recruited by another prestigious law firm, and she remains a partner there today. Although fully established in her career and the lead partner in her area, she still works extremely long days. She rises at five A.M., swims for at least an hour, and then heads to the office. Most days she stays there until nine at night. She works almost every weekend but takes the occasional afternoon off to play golf. She also enjoys traveling, participating in various charities, and investing in art and other collectibles. Whatever she undertakes, she applies herself with discipline.

It is a rich life, richly lived, and Donna's greatest financial worry is whether she will be able to maintain it in the style to which she has become accustomed. Twenty years from now she still hopes to be traveling, doing charity work, buying art, and golfing. "Life cannot be only about work," Donna says. She anticipates receiving retirement benefits from her law firm, but her early experience—plus the recent failure of such corporate giants as Arthur Andersen—remind her that there is no hard and fast guarantee about such benefits or about anything else.

Her investments are conservative yet somewhat random. She has not reached out to any financial advisors because she's not sure that she could trust one. Nor does she follow an overall strategy. Instead, Donna maintains investments in various accounts at multiple institutions. She does not spend a lot of time thinking about her investments, although she thinks she should devote more attention to the whole issue.

Donna is convinced that at some point in her life, she will sit down and figure out a financial plan. Right now, however, the current approach seems fine. For one thing, it's hard to think about changing the approach when her income is so significant and her assets so substantial. She knows that she has no worries about being provided for, and that she has the means to continue to accumulate assets.

Moreover, although she contributes to the support and education of some family members, and while she expects that the plan she will one day devise will include leaving legacies for the charities to which she now contributes substantially, Donna does not have a spouse or a family of her own. In a sense, it's all hers, and in the midst of such plenty, it's hard to see the necessity of changing her ways.

She is the perfect candidate for creating a financial plan and following a methodology.

A PORTRAIT OF PERPETUAL WEALTH: HOW TO DO IT RIGHT

Jon O'Malley has lived the success story of immigrant America. He came to the United States at the age of eighteen. He knew no one in New York, his port of call, but he was able to bunk with a friend of a friend. Because Jon had been bartending in his native Ireland since the age of eleven, he felt he knew the business, and within two weeks he got a job as a bartender in Manhattan.

He began to save his money. In his own words, "I saved every nickel"—enough, after a few years, for Jon to buy a bar of his own. He not only bought the bar business, he also bought the building. The bar became extremely successful because the area in which it was located was just beginning to become popular with one of Manhattan's trendier crowds. This also greatly increased the value of the real estate Jon had been smart enough to buy.

Today, Jon O'Malley owns four bars in trendy areas of Manhattan. Each area is different, and Jon has made sure to make each bar different. Striking out in a new direction, he has also just opened his first restaurant. He is a wealthy man.

He acknowledges that he has a knack for spotting developing neighborhoods but also attributes his success to "hard work and good fortune." He owes "not a dime" and remains extremely frugal, continuing to save routinely. Jon and his wife and their young children live over one of the bars that he owns—it's his own building as well—and they recently bought a weekend house near the beach.

It hasn't all been smooth sailing. One of Jon O'Malley's bars is across the street from a firehouse that lost a number of firemen on September 11, 2001. That bar, along with the others, had lighter than normal business for the months after 9/11, and the downturn made 2001 Jon's first nongrowth year. The loss of the firemen and the blow to New York, a city Jon has grown to love, were, of course, far worse than the financial reverses;

the bar business came back, but the firemen of course never did.

What is Jon working *for*? One of his financial goals is to be able to finance his children's college education. He completed only high school and believes that education is an important gift. He knows that he will be able to accomplish this goal, and perhaps senses that the wealth he has gained is sufficient to be passed on to his own children and to future generations as well.

The real estate holdings and the consistent innovation of this entrepreneur are twin engines of ongoing wealth; buttressed by his savings and investments, he will easily meet his goal to retire or semiretire at age fifty—unless he wants to keep on going.

Jon arrived here with no prospects and the single skill of being able to mix a cocktail, and today he is rich enough to stay rich for the rest of his life and pass his wealth on to multiple future generations. The secrets were there. Jon O'Malley uncovered them.

CHAPTER 10

PASSING IT ON: ENSURING YOUR MONEY GOES ON BEYOND YOU

Here's the story of two sons, Joe and Dan, and their fathers. Joe's father owned a business that made exhibits for trade shows. Headquartered in a suburb of a city known for conventions, the business boomed. When Joe graduated from college, he immediately went to work for his father's firm—at just the time that his father decided to retire. To fund the retirement, Joe Sr. sold the business for several million dollars to a competitor. Joe Jr. discovered that it was mighty uncomfortable working for the new owners, so his father helped him find a job at yet another competitor's business; at least it was a similar type of company—one that dealt in exhibits.

Meanwhile, Joe Sr. and Mrs. Joe Sr. took the proceeds of the sale, moved into a delightful home in Florida, bought a big boat, and sailed into the sunset. Twenty years later, most of the assets have been spent. Joe Jr. meanwhile keeps moving from exhibit company to exhibit company trying to find the right spot—or to at least hold onto a job.

Joe's friend, Dan, had a father with an entirely different approach. Dan Sr. owned a couple of stores that specialized in selling paint, glass, and wallpaper. When Dan graduated from college, he went to work for his father, starting out as a clerk in one of his father's stores. With time and experience, Dan moved up to manage the store—and eventually, to manage the company.

Dan Sr., however, never really retired; in fact, to this day, he still draws a salary from the business, although he is rarely in the office. Instead, he sails, flies airplanes, competes in tennis tournaments, and travels with his wife all around the world. Dan Jr. remains in charge of the company, which, by the way, he has expanded into a quasi-empire of 20 stores across two states.

In addition, Dan Jr. and Sr. have together invested in multiple properties both for the store as well as for their personal fortunes: vacation homes, apartment buildings, and office buildings. For Dan Sr. and Mrs. Dan Sr., these "golden days" are particularly radiant because they not only enjoy their retirement, they also know they have ensured that their children and grandchildren will be protected for many generations.

Sometimes, over a beer, Dan and Joe discuss how differently life has turned out for each of them. On one side at least, it's not a very happy conversation.

The moral of the story is this: Understand what you're wishing for when you say you wish to pass on your wealth; know exactly how you want future generations to benefit.

To put this moral in perspective, let's assume that by now you have done what this book recommends and have achieved perpetual wealth. You have invested in real estate and are receiving an ongoing income stream from your properties. You have grown your own business and invested in other innovative enterprises that continue to renew and refresh the springs of your wealth. You know that you will be comfortable during your retirement and will be able to live the lifestyle of your choice. You know there is enough wealth to ensure comfort and security for those who come after you.

But having enough isn't the same as structuring your legacy to do what you intend it to do. So the question becomes: What can you do to make sure that your heirs will be protected once you are gone—or to ensure that the cause you support will be able to receive the benefits of your legacy? In short, how can you be sure you're passing on the wealth you've achieved in the way you want it to be passed on?

Part of the answer is to consult with advisors of various types: lawyers, accountants, trust officers, and possibly investment managers. But before you pick up the phone to call any one of those professionals, you must first determine what it is you want to achieve. How, exactly, do you want to pass on your wealth? What, exactly, do you want your wealth to do for your heirs? What is the legacy you want to leave? Once you've answered those questions, the lawyers and accountants and other professionals can determine the best way to implement your objectives, at which point they can come up with what is essentially an estate plan.

Without such a plan, you run the risk of having your assets dissipated by estate taxes and divvied up in a way you did not determine—a way that may not work out well for your family.

For example, suppose you're the parent of a daughter and son. Your son has shown no interest in the business you built from scratch—the business that was the main engine of your considerable fortune. But while your son is planning a career in scientific research, your daughter is gung-ho to move right into the boardroom and is even now applying to business school. You've pretty well decided that you'd like her to take over the business some day, but of course you want also to split your financial legacy equally between the two children. How will you work that out? If you "give" the business to your daughter, does that then justify leaving more of your real estate properties to your son? Will you bequeath the business to your daughter in shares of stock or through some other mechanism? When should you act?

All of these questions can be answered, with the help of experts, once you've answered the "life" question—that the business will go to your daughter—and only then. That's when the professionals can help you structure the terms of a legacy that meets both your desire to keep the business in the family through your daughter and your objective of dividing your wealth equally between the two children.

So ask yourself these questions at a minimum:

- Do you want to fund your grandchildren's college education?

- Do you want to assist your children or grandchildren in buying real estate of their own? A first home? A rental property?

- Do you want to fund an annual scholarship at your alma mater—perhaps for a student interested in your favorite hobby or your business or some kind of research?

- What about contributing to your favorite local charities—the Boy Scouts or Girl Scouts? The church? The food shelter?

- Do you want to pass your company on to your daughter or son?

Let the questions suggest similar topics for you to think about as you determine how you want to pass on the wealth you've achieved.

PLANNING YOUR LEGACY

The goals for passing on wealth to one's heirs are as varied as the individuals themselves—with all their idiosyncrasies.

Yes, the most common goal, expressed by 60 percent of the wealthy, is to maximize the amount left to their children. But our research has found that 58 percent also want to avoid estate taxes; 27 percent want to reduce family conflict; 26 percent want to facilitate gifts to charity; 15 percent want to ensure a successful business transition; and 16 percent have not yet decided what they want to do with their assets.

The research also shows that 78 percent of wealthy households not only know where they want their wealth to go, they are confident that they have an effective plan in place to get it there. Only 7 percent don't have a plan in place, while the rest aren't actually sure.

But the fact is that the high percentage of wealthy households confident that they have set up a plan of action are kidding themselves. For most of them, "having a plan of action" means only that they have made out a will. It does not mean that they have worked with a professional estate planner or that they have established any type of trust vehicle to shelter their assets from taxes and pass them to the next generation safely, securely, and effectively.

Millionaire and Mega-Millionaire "Estate Planning"

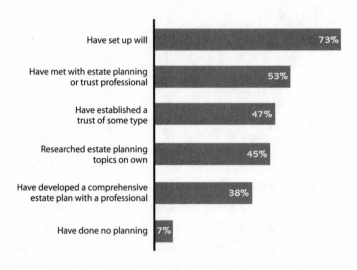

So what type of planning—beyond your last will and testament—should you put in place? Here's where you need to call on the professionals. If, as we've assumed, you've applied the secrets this book puts in your hands—or plan to—your estate planning is going to require a lot more than just a will.

Different wealthy households use different types of estate planning tools—often a range of them for different purposes. This is why you need professional assistance: The tool that makes most sense for you is the one that best answers your personal objectives, and only you can best judge what those are.

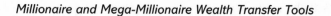

Millionaire and Mega-Millionaire Wealth Transfer Tools

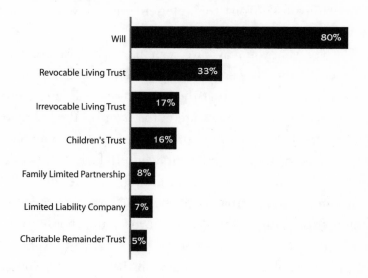

Start by talking to your lawyer and accountant, as always. See what they think, ask what they recommend. Their professional expertise can help you use the right tool for the job of structuring your legacy your way.

TRUSTS

It's not unlikely that you'll determine that a trust is the right vehicle. We know it's not unlikely because our research shows that forty-one percent of wealthy households have a trust in place today, with many more set to establish a trust as they age. Once the trust is established, about 62 percent of these households' total assets are placed in trust.

Does this mean that you will have to negotiate with a

serious-looking individual in a suit every time a financial decision is called for? Won't this interfere with how you want to live your life?

Despite what you may have seen in movies based on Dickens's novels, the answer is no, absolutely not. The only real hassle will be ensuring that the titles of your various properties, stocks, and other assets are in the name of the trust. Your attorney can help you with that. Otherwise, it is common for you to act as the trustee until your death. In fact, 74 percent of individuals trustee their own trust during their lifetime.

Moreover, you can name the individual or organization you want as trustee upon your death. Maybe you'll choose to have your bank's trust department act as your trustee to work with your family to distribute and maintain the assets. Or you can name your brother, your daughter, your lawyer (only in some states), or a family friend to act as trustee upon your death—if you so choose. Whomever you name, that person will work in conjunction with the bank; in other words, the bank will maintain custody of the assets, but your appointed trustee will direct the activity of the assets.

ESTATE PLANNING: A CAUTIONARY TALE

Jonathan, a widower, owned a business that provided adjusting and accounting services to various insurance companies. While the business had been highly successful, Jonathan had experienced profound tragedy in his personal life. After struggling with cancer for many years, his wife had died young, leaving Jonathan to raise their five children. Despite the challenges, all five children grew to be successful adults with successful careers; three of them, in fact, worked for the family business.

Yet Jonathan almost never discussed financial or personal issues with his family. It was part of his Irish upbringing, which taught him that personal matters were to be kept personal—held close to the vest. He didn't even want to consult with an attorney about his assets. So when Jonathan died at a ripe old age, there was virtually nothing in the way of estate planning to guide his heirs. The bulk of his assets were tied up in a very large IRA account—rolled over from a defined benefit plan that had been terminated by his business— and everything else was in his own name. It meant that the children had to work effectively together to ensure that the assets were properly distributed and to try to avoid as many estate taxes as possible.

They weren't very successful. The real sticking point was that the IRA was invested in bonds. While all five children agreed they should place the IRA assets in investments promising higher returns, they all had to agree on which money manager to use. Despite their maturity and theoretical good will, this was a recipe for disaster. Jonathan's heirs couldn't agree and the money stayed in bonds; everybody, including Jonathan, the diligent single father of five successful children, lost out.

CHAPTER 11

A QUICK REVIEW OF THE SECRETS OF PERPETUAL WEALTH

You *are* richer than you think. And you now have the tools to get still richer: to both stay rich for your lifetime and to pass your wealth on to multiple future generations.

How and where do you start? How do you turn the model into reality? How do you apply the principles and practices we've discussed to your particular situation? After all, you're about to undertake a program of real change. It will work best and go most smoothly if you attend to a few housekeeping details first.

For openers, you'd be well advised to clear the decks financially speaking. That means paying off all your credit card debt and resolving any other financial loose ends so that you're starting with a clean slate. It's interesting and instructive to note that the perpetually wealthy use credit cards routinely—just about daily, in fact—but they pay off their balance each month. It's a good habit to get into, and it's a basic requirement for starting your personal program to get rich, stay rich, and pass it on.

Second, do you own your primary residence? If not, buying it should be the first objective in your program for creating money forever. It is, in a sense, another component of clearing the decks so you have a clean slate to write on. Chapter 5 gives you all the details you need to know to make that purchase; think of it as the first step to the kind of wealth that keeps on paying back for generations to come.

Third, start opening your eyes to the entrepreneurial opportunities around you. Sometimes it's just a matter of shifting your mind-set slightly so that you look at the familiar with fresh eyes. When you do, suddenly the boarded-up, rundown movie theater downtown looks like a fabulous, combination indie-film theater–coffee shop–art gallery–Internet café that would cater to both the college kids and the many young professionals moving into the area. Then maybe you could find some investors who would be as interested as you are in a Chinese restaurant in the empty building next door. The point is to think in terms of new enterprises—until you see them everywhere, even in old failures.

Fourth, start a regular savings plan. We are not telling you that if you give up the daily latte and instead put the money into a milk jar, the miracle of compound interest will make you a mega-millionaire in one day. Nor are we saying that wearing secondhand suits and driving only used cars will make you rich enough to stay rich for a lifetime and pass the wealth on. What we *can* say is that regular savings provide a pool from which to draw money for the kinds of investments that repay income for a lifetime. It's a good thing to do, and if you're not doing it, you'd be wise to start.

Fifth, don't neglect the other categories—marketable securities, life insurance and annuities, retirement plans, and other investments—as you begin to match your current asset allocation to the benchmark model, focusing on real estate investment and engaging in continually innovative enterprises. Well managed, preferably with the help of expert advisors, such investments can provide valuable returns.

Sixth and finally, keep in mind that all of this is doable. You really can get rich enough to stay rich for your lifetime and pass your wealth on to your heirs for generations and generations into the future. This book has uncovered the secrets for doing so and put them into your hands. Take a good grip, and go get rich forever.

APPENDIX

SECRETS OF THE WEALTHY REVEALED

Want more facts about how the rich get rich, stay rich, and pass it on?

Here are 13 sets of cold, hard figures that embody the wealth-accumulation secrets of America's richest families. The numbers add color to the picture this book has painted of just how the mega-millionaires get and stay rich enough to pass it on.

These data are ours alone. We remain a unique source of information about wealthy households and those on the way to becoming wealthy. It is why we also remain a unique resource for the financial industry and for economists in a range of organizations who want to understand where these households get their money, how they invest it, what kinds of returns those investments yield, and what factors influence the financial decisions the members of these households make on a daily, weekly, or yearly basis.

We get the answers to these questions by layering several levels of research; these levels both confirm and complement one another to produce a three-dimensional picture of the nation's richest families.

First, we research these households month after month after month. That way, we can see emerging patterns and can take note of any shifts in the patterns or deviations from them. Then, on an annual basis, we survey some 5,000 wealthy households—including the mass affluent, millionaires, and mega-millionaires. Finally, we support the data this research yields not only with online research and literature searches, but by holding focus groups on a regular basis all around the country. These focus groups are like the essay question on college exams. Remember? While the multiple-choice questions focused on unequivocal facts, the essay question offered a chance to penetrate beyond the facts to experience and interpretation. That's what the focus groups give us as well—and they thus help us understand the how and why as well as the what of wealth accumulation.

In writing this book, we've added yet another layer of research—namely, in-depth interviews with dozens of wealthy individuals, many of whom you have met in person in the body of the book.

This appendix concentrates on the unequivocal facts that define the baseline of wealth accumulation in the United States today, leavened by some of that enriching interview research. The tables that follow will tell you where America's richest families get their wealth and where they put it. We'll drill down from total assets to marketable assets and then to each category of investment, showing you where and how much the rich invest in stocks and bonds, mutual funds, alternative investments, real estate, and retirement plans.

The data also tell a good deal more about the financial behavior of America's richest families. You'll see how and why advisors are used, just how much the rich save, the financial goals they express, and how they respond when it comes to donating to charity.

The bottom line is a model, drawn in numbers, of getting rich, staying rich, and passing it on. Use it to write your own prescription for perpetual wealth.

WHERE DO AMERICA'S RICHEST FAMILIES GET THEIR WEALTH?

Mega-millionaires—investors with over $5 million of net worth not including their primary residence—receive 43 percent of their annual income from investments and only 40 percent from salary. This is in comparison to mass affluent investors, whose net worth is between $100,000 to $1 million (not including their primary residence), who receive 57 percent of their annual income from salary and only 20 percent from investments. The goal is to increase your investment income.

Mega-Millionaires—Source of Household Income

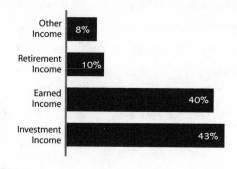

Mass Affluent—Source of Household Income

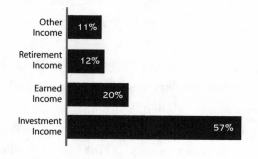

WHERE DO THEY PUT IT?

Less than half of mega-millionaires' assets are invested in marketable assets whose value fluctuates daily with the market. Investment real estate and privately held business represent more than 35 percent of their total assets.

Distribution of Total Assets—Mega-Millionaires

HOW DO THE RICH ALLOCATE
THEIR MARKETABLE ASSETS?

The 40 to 45 percent of the mega-millionaire's assets that are marketable securities are allocated across a number of investment types.

Distribution of Marketable Assets—Mega-Millionaires

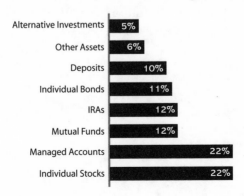

Managed Accounts

Many mega-millionaires hire the types of advisors discussed in Chapter 8 to manage a portion of their assets in what is commonly referred to as a managed account.

Other Assets

Other assets include commodities, futures, collectibles, limited partnerships, charitable gift funds, and structured products.

Alternative Investments

Alternative investments include hedge funds, private placements, private equity, and venture capital.

HOW MUCH DO THE RICH PUT
INTO STOCKS AND BONDS?

The average amount invested in individual stocks and bonds by mega-millionaires is broken out in the accompanying chart.

Stocks and Bonds—Mega-Millionaires
Average Balance ($000s)

HOW MUCH GOES INTO MUTUAL FUNDS?

The mega-millionaires' average balance invested in various types of mutual funds is shown in the accompanying chart.

Mutual Funds—Mega-Millionaires
Average Balance ($000s)

WHAT ABOUT "ALTERNATIVE" INVESTMENTS?
WHO INVESTS IN THEM—AND HOW MUCH?

The percent of mega-millionaires that own various types of alternative investments, and their average balances, are outlined in the two charts shown.

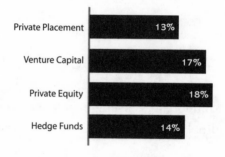

Alternative Investments—Mega-Millionaires
Percent Owning

Private Placement — 13%
Venture Capital — 17%
Private Equity — 18%
Hedge Funds — 14%

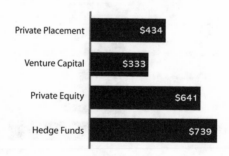

Alternative Investments—Mega-Millionaires
Average Balance ($000s)

Private Placement — $434
Venture Capital — $333
Private Equity — $641
Hedge Funds — $739

UNLOCKING THE REAL ESTATE INVESTMENT SECRET: WHAT DO THE RICH INVEST IN AND WHAT'S THE VALUE OF THEIR INVESTMENTS?

The percent of mega-millionaires who own various types of investment real estate, and the average market values, are identified in the charts shown.

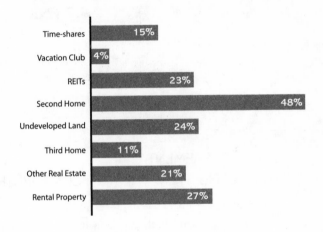

Investment Real Estate—Mega-Millionaires Ownership

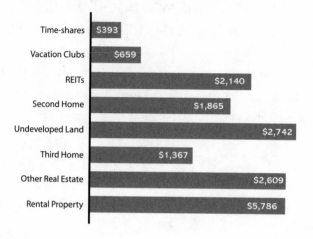

Investment Real Estate—Mega-Millionaires
Average Market Value ($000s)

- Time-shares: $393
- Vacation Clubs: $659
- REITs: $2,140
- Second Home: $1,865
- Undeveloped Land: $2,742
- Third Home: $1,367
- Other Real Estate: $2,609
- Rental Property: $5,786

RETIREMENT PLANS:
WHAT AND HOW MUCH DO THE RICH CONTRIBUTE?

Mega-millionaires contribute to their employer-sponsored retirement plans to a great extent. They also take advantage of the tax benefits of Roth IRAs and, to the extent available, contributory IRAs. Rollover IRAs are created when an investor retires or changes jobs and transfers his or her retirement assets from the employer's retirement plan, such as a 401(k), to an IRA.

Retirement Accounts—Mega-Millionaires
Percent Owning

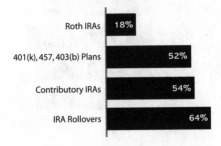

Roth IRAs — 18%
401(k), 457, 403(b) Plans — 52%
Contributory IRAs — 54%
IRA Rollovers — 64%

Retirement Accounts—$25M+
Average Balance ($000s)

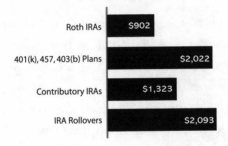

Roth IRAs — $902
401(k), 457, 403(b) Plans — $2,022
Contributory IRAs — $1,323
IRA Rollovers — $2,093

WHO USES PROFESSIONAL FINANCIAL ADVISORS?

Almost three-quarters of mega-millionaire households use a primary professional advisor. That usage does not vary dramatically by age.

Mega-Millionaires—Primary Financial Advisor Usage

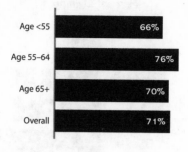

HOW DO THEY USE THEM?

About two-thirds of mega-millionaires use an advisor that is affiliated with a large financial services firm. Thirty percent use an independent advisor, or one that is not affiliated with a large firm. Those who use independent advisors often do so because they perceive they are more objective. Today advisors of all types are expected to recommend investments from multiple firms, not just their own.

Mega-Millionaire—Advisor Usage
Affiliated or Unaffiliated Advisors

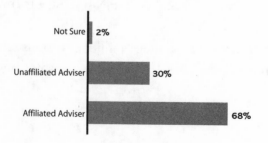

THE RICH SAVE MORE.

Mega-millionaire households have very high savings rates compared to the average savings rates of U.S. households.

Mega-Millionaires—Savings Rate

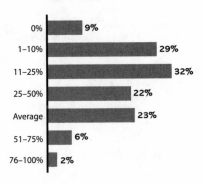

THE RICH SHARE THE FINANCIAL GOALS
EXPRESSED BY MOST AMERICANS.

The financial goals of mega-millionaires are very similar to those of most American households.

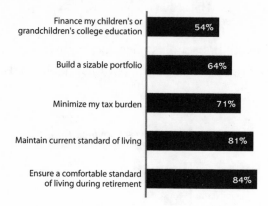

Mega-Millionaires—Financial Goals

Finance my children's or grandchildren's college education	54%
Build a sizable portfolio	64%
Minimize my tax burden	71%
Maintain current standard of living	81%
Ensure a comfortable standard of living during retirement	84%

THE RICH GIVE GENEROUSLY.

Mega-millionaire households are most likely to make donations to religious organizations, followed by schools, educational organizations, and social service organizations.

Mega-Millionaires—Charitable Giving

Religious	College/ School	Social Service Organizations	Hospital, Health Care, Curative	Arts, Cultural, Humanities	Other	Disaster Relief	Environmental
30%	17%	17%	10%	9%	7%	6%	4%

ACKNOWLEDGMENTS

Accustomed as we are to professional collaboration, the creation of *Get Rich, Stay Rich, Pass It On* afforded us teamwork of a whole different order of magnitude, and we are grateful for the chance here to acknowledge and thank those who gave us so much help and encouragement.

Our thanks first to the first movers of the book, Farrell Kramer and Sharon Bially of Farrell Kramer Communications. They persuaded us that the story we had to tell deserved a wider audience. Moreover, through Sharon, we found Susanna Margolis, who provided valuable editorial assistance in turning our descriptive data into prescriptive prose.

We are grateful to Lindsay Edgecombe at the Levine Greenberg Literary Agency and of course to our agent, Jim Levine. Lindsay was the first representative of the publishing industry to give our idea a professional nod of approval, and Jim and all the folks at Levine Greenberg provided consistent support, bolstered our confidence, and were helpful and attentive throughout. Jim is the finest guide to the world of publishing a pair of novices could hope for.

At Portfolio, we extend thanks to Adrian Zackheim, Jeffrey Krames, and their team of Courtney Young, Will Weisser, and Allison Sweet for "getting" our message and for helping us get it out there loud and clear. Jeff Krames exhibited uncanny skill in coaxing the best out of us, while holding our hands every step of the way. We are indebted to him for the skill, the coaxing, the hand-holding, and his persistent good cheer in making this book a reality.

We could not have managed the process of writing the book without the talented and conscientious help of our Spectrem colleague, Tom Wynn, master researcher of the affluent market.

We would be remiss if we did not offer thanks, albeit "anonymously," to the thousands of mass affluent, millionaires, and mega-millionaires who submitted to our scrutiny and provided the data on which *Get Rich, Stay Rich, Pass It On* is based. We offer particular thanks to those individuals who shared with us the details of their personal as well as financial lives.

Finally, we are grateful to our families for their encouragement and for putting up with our frequent travel and long hours. If you've always wondered just what it is we do at work, now you know.

ONLINE RESOURCES

You can find additional resources for achieving perpetual wealth at our Web site, www.millionairecorner.com.

Features include:

- Wealth tips of the week

- Additional insights on how to get rich, stay rich, pass it on

- Tips for developing business plans

- Insights on creating a real estate investment plan

- Strategies for developing innovative enterprises

- Financial planning guidance

- The *Millionaire Corner* monthly newsletter

INDEX